# ACCESS
# TO THE
# WORLD

"Invaluable information for handicapped travelers and their families."—*Dallas News*

"An excellent, informative book."
—*Cincinnati Post*

"An exceptionally interesting and valuable book, not to be missed."—*Manchester Union Leader*

# ACCESS TO THE WORLD

## A TRAVEL GUIDE FOR THE HANDICAPPED

Louise Weiss

An Owl Book
Henry Holt and Company | New York

*Collected Poems* by W. H. Auden, edited by Edward Mendelson,
copyright © 1940, and renewed 1968 by W. H. Auden.
Published by Random House, Inc.

Published by Henry Holt and Company, Inc.,
521 Fifth Avenue, New York, New York 10175.
Published simultaneously in Canada.

Library of Congress Cataloging-in-Publication Data
Weiss, Louise.
Access to the world.
"An Owl book."
Includes index.
1. Physically handicapped—Travel—Handbooks, manuals,
etc. 2. Handicapped—Travel—Handbooks, manuals, etc.
I. Title.
HV3022.W44   1983b      910'.240816      85–27354
ISBN 0-8050-0141-7 (pbk.)

First published in hardcover by Chatham Square Press in 1977; second edition
published in hardcover by Facts on File, Inc., in 1983.

First Owl Book Edition—1986

Printed in the United States of America
1   3   5   7   9   10   8   6   4   2

ISBN 0-8050-0141-7

*In loving memory of Norman and Janet Wilkes*

Dreamed I saw a building with a thousand floors,
A thousand windows and a thousand doors;
Not one of them was ours, my dear, not one of them was ours.

—W. H. Auden
*Collected Poems*

I will find a way or I will make one.

—Hannibal, circa 218 B.C., referring
to the passage through the Alps

# CONTENTS

# PREFACE

When I first told people I was planning to write a book about travel for the handicapped, I got a lot of widely varying reactions.

"Do they ever travel?"

"What a worthy thing to do!"

"I suppose travel agents know all about it anyway."

"Don't all the airlines have the same rules?"

"But there aren't any problems. Someone will always help."

"They never travel alone, do they?"

Which goes to show that people often have strange ideas about those they don't know very well. Many may not think they have a handicapped person among their friends or relatives, although anybody who knows a diabetic, a heart-attack victim, or a dialysis patient knows a handicapped person. Just as these people make every effort to lead normal lives, to work and to play like everyone else, so too do paraplegics, quadriplegics, amputees, post-polios, and sufferers from such diseases as muscular dystrophy, multiple sclerosis, and cerebral palsy. Mainly, they are confined to wheelchairs, which create enormous logistical problems in maneuvering up, down, and through our stair-studded obstacle course of a world. The wheelchair is indeed a problem, but the person in the chair is an individual who wants to live his or her life as fully and competently as the rest of us do—more so, perhaps, because such a person may have greater reason to be thankful for simply being alive.

Yes, indeed, handicapped people travel. They make business trips on the Boston–New York–Washington shuttles and on the red-eye special coast to coast. They travel on buses and trains to see the Grand Canyon and Washington, D.C., visit relatives, or go on a holiday outing. They fly to London and Paris to take in all the sights. They go to conventions in Australia, they go to see the Pope in Rome, they go on safari in Kenya. And just because they are disabled, they are not necessarily poor. Many are middle-class working people, some are wealthy, but even the less well-off may participate in organizations that have funds to enrich their lives with some amount of travel.

The first thing you learn when you start talking to handicapped people (some prefer the term *disabled*) is that they don't want sympathy or charity. They want to be able to do things as normally as possible and as much as possible *for themselves*. Widening a door, making curb cuts in a sidewalk, adding a ramp next to a stairway—these are things that allow them to go where they want on their own in daily life and on vacation.

It's true that travel agents know about a lot of things, but travel for the handicapped isn't one of them. Except for a minuscule number of agents and tour operators who have been specialists in the field for a long time, there is little understanding of the needs of disabled travelers or knowledge of the facilities that are available and accessible to them. Recently, more and more agents have become aware of the situation. Many of them are eager, in fact, to employ their professional skills in serving a segment of the traveling public that has been largely invisible up to now, but they need specific information in order to do their best for handicapped clients.

No, the airlines don't all have the same rules. Each line has its own policy developed by trial and error over the years, and there are marked differences among them. Buses are different. Trains are different. Ships are another story. Hotels, restaurants, theaters, theme parks—think of a place to go and you'll find problems for the handicapped, but fortunately, more and more bright spots are emerging.

"Someone will always help" falls under the category of famous last words. The someone is usually a little old lady under the illusion that she can get a 150-pound man in a 40-pound wheelchair through a door that is two inches narrower than the chair. There are times when "someone" helping is very useful and much appreciated, but it is not to be counted on. As one man confined to a wheelchair commented, "If I waited for someone to push me up and down high curbs, I'd be on the same street corner for ten years." It's easier to remove the barrier than to count on the appearance of a good Samaritan.

Since being alone seems to be an increasingly common condition of modern man, why should a handicapped person be any different? Even a mate is unlikely to be available twenty-four hours a day. And a single adult, handicapped or not, whether he lives alone or not, wants to go places by himself. He may prefer to have friends along on a vacation, as anyone might, but if he is independent-minded and self-reliant, he is not going to give up a holiday because there's no one available to go with him.

Thus, it should be obvious that handicapped people are

just like everyone else, except that they have to work harder to enjoy many of the pleasures and satisfactions of life. Mobility is an essential component of the world today and it is as much a component of leisure as it is of work. Handicapped people want to achieve as much mobility as they are capable of so that they can lead the freest, most independent, and most enjoyable lives they are capable of.

# ACKNOWLEDGMENTS

A book as diverse in its scope as this one could not have been written without the help and cooperation of people from many walks of life. I am grateful to everyone who contributed some measure of information or expertise to my research, but there are some I would like to mention for special thanks and appreciation:

My editors, Peter Bejger and Joseph Reilly, for their patience and expertise; David Harrop for encouragement and support; and the late Norman Wilkes for unfailing help and friendship that will be sadly missed.

Carr Massi, Ralph Eckelman and Robert Eichel of the New York Metropolitan Chapter of the National Paraplegia Foundation; Jean-Claude Barré; Dr. Monique Fol; Joni Eareckson; Patricia Hughes; and Roy Andries de Groot—all of whom gave me some insight into the world of the handicapped traveler.

Dr. Thomas Jones, director of the International Health Care Service of The New York Hospital-Cornell Medical Center, and Paula White of Harbor Nephrology Associates for advice on health aspects of travel.

Marguerite Allen, Georgia Beach, Steven Pisni, and many other good friends for contributing their knowledge of special areas of the travel industry.

Lord Snowdon for graciously contributing the introduction to this book in keeping with his long-standing interest and involvement in helping the handicapped enter the mainstream of life.

Finally, I owe a special debt of gratitude to the late Lee Foster of *The New York Times*, who enthusiastically confirmed the need for a travel guide for the handicapped and encouraged me to embark on writing the first edition of this book in the hope, sadly unfulfilled, that he would be one of its first readers.

# INTRODUCTION

Since 1981, the International Year of Disabled People, it has been encouraging to see the considerable improvements that have been made in the availability of facilities for handicapped people. In the English-speaking countries especially, there has been a remarkable heightening of awareness that a physical disability is an impediment to be overcome, not a stigma to provoke embarrassment or shame. Perhaps the greatest accomplishment of 1981 was the recognition of how much more remains to be done; so much so, in fact, that 1983–1992 has become the United Nations Decade of Disabled Persons. We must not lose the opportunity to make certain that we are at the start of a new era of understanding for the benefit of disabled people.

"Accessibility," of course, has been one of the watchwords of our endeavours. We want as many people as possible to be able to go where they want and do what they want without stumbling over barriers, great or small, that serve to shut them out from the occasions of normal life. But not all the barriers are physical ones. Architectural modifications are frequently so easy to make that we may be tempted to think that that is all there is to it. In reality, it is the mental and emotional barriers that so often keep people from recognizing their mutual humanity.

Whenever the able-bodied avert their eyes from the wheelchair-bound, or speak about the blind as though they lacked hearing, too, or assume that deaf means "dumb" in the colloquial sense, then there is a barrier that will keep the able-bodied and the handicapped from relating to one another in the normal modes of everyday life. This is detrimental to both, for they are equally cut off from potentially enriching social, intellectual, and emotional relationships because of differences in physical capability.

Travel, a major component of modern society for work, study, and recreation, is an aspect of life that has only recently begun to be opened up to the handicapped. It is mainly in Britain and North America that this has occurred, so that now one often sees adventurous Americans, Canadians, and Britons of all ages and with all sorts of physical disabilities experiencing the same pleasures of foreign and domestic travel as their more able-bodied contemporaries, although frequently encountering more discomforts.

As these pioneers lead the way for others into the mainstream of society, it is my hope that the mainstream will embrace them with a warm welcome, not only with consideration for their disabilities but also with respect for their abilities. *Access to the World* will, I hope, be of great help and guidance to disabled people for charting a course into a new world of pleasure and fulfillment.

The Right Honourable
The Earl of Snowdon, GCVO
President for England of the
International Year of Disabled People

# 1

# AIR TRAVEL

The airlines might be startled to hear this but, at least from one point of view, handicapped people are ideal air travelers because there is hardly a white knuckle among them. Not one of the many people I interviewed expressed anything but complete confidence in the skill and competence of the crews and the mechanical efficiency of the equipment. One and all, they simply said, "No, I'm not afraid." Many said, "I know that flying is far safer than driving a car and I drive my hand-controlled car in heavy traffic every day." And they mean it. It seems to be only the able-bodied who require hypnosis, group therapy, tranquilizers, or several stiff drinks in order to endure the anxiety of becoming airborne.

The airlines, on the other hand, have achieved their enviable safety records by worrying constantly about every factor that might affect their desired goal—uneventful, punctual, comfortable takeoffs, flights, and landings. To this end, they worry about crew training, they worry about equipment, and they worry about passengers. As a result, relations between airlines and handicapped travelers have long had some love—hate aspects. On the one hand, airlines like to collect fares and fill up empty seats. They also like to reinforce their image as public-service organizations by making heroic efforts to cope with extraordinary situations and provide the kind of service that makes people feel they're dealing with a warm human being instead of a corporate automaton. But—they're still worrying about safety (and if they aren't, the Federal Aviation Administration [FAA] is doing it for them).

Over the years the individual airlines have established their own criteria for the carriage of handicapped people in conformity with a provision of the Federal Aviation Act of 1958 that permits airlines to deny passage to anyone whose presence might be "inimical" to flight safety. This is the provision that lets the captain throw an obnoxious drunk off the plane, to no one's great distress except the drunk's. But it also has led to some thoughtless and inadvertently callous treatment of the handicapped.

Handicapped people have objected most vigorously to the requirement of some airlines for medical certificates—frequently calling not only for a new certificate for each flight but even for separate certificates for *each leg* of one flight. On some international trips, passengers have been called off the plane at *every* stop to get the approval of an airline physician. Some opponents feel as strongly as Carr Massi of the New York Metropolitan Chapter of the National Paraplegia Foundation (NPF). Massi says: "If I have to get a letter from a doctor, all the other passengers should, too. Who says an able-bodied person isn't going to panic in an emergency?" Others, like Bob Eichel, a former travel agent and an active member of the NPF, don't object to the certificate in principle but think there should be only one required with a reasonably long period of validity, or, even better, an identification card that would once and for all eliminate any question of a person's ability to travel.

Many handicapped people believe that the requirement for a constantly renewed medical certificate indicates a misunderstanding on the part of some airlines of the difference between what the Air Traffic Conference of America defines as "static" and "non-static" ambulatory and non-ambulatory conditions. A static ambulatory condition, for example, would be blindness. A non-static ambulatory passenger might be someone who has just undergone surgery or had a heart attack but is capable of walking short distances. "Non-static, non-ambulatory" would describe all stretcher cases as well as seriously ill people who require a wheelchair. And finally there is "static non-ambulatory," which is applied to paraplegia, quadriplegia, post-polio, and any other condition that keeps a healthy person confined to a wheelchair because he or she can't walk.

Actually, there is a card available now that addresses these problems and at least partially alleviates them. A person with a *stable* handicapping condition can obtain a Frequent Traveller's Medical Card (FREMEC), which eliminates the need for medical clearance for each trip. All airlines that are members of the International Air Transport Association will honor the FREMEC as medical clearance, subject to any limitations indicated on the card. IATA members include most, but not all, major foreign and domestic lines. The cards are issued by the medical departments of the individual airlines. Be forewarned: many airline personnel have never heard of the card. Persistence in getting through to a medical department that does issue the card will be rewarded, however, by decreasing inconvenience for frequent travelers.

That is certainly the key to a lot of misunderstanding. Many people who can't walk are healthy and otherwise perfectly normal. The helpful ground hostess says, "You'll just have to walk a few steps, then you can get back into your chair."

"But I can't walk at all," replies Carr Massi. "That's why I'm in a wheelchair." It is very difficult for many people to grasp the difference between those who can't walk very far (heart patients, for instance) and those who can't walk at all. Sickness and disability are two different things and disabled people find it offensive and insulting to be treated as though they were sick.

Another sore point has been the matter of traveling unaccompanied. Some carriers specify unequivocally that "any passenger unable to move around freely or to attend to his personal requirements . . . must be accompanied by a capable attendant." In actual practice, however, most lines are flexible and prefer to use such terms as "when dependent," "at discretion of physician," or "at discretion of airline."

However, the term "attendant," with its connotation of sickness and physical and mental incapacity, is distressing to a person in a wheelchair who may very well drive to work every day, put in a full day at the office or factory, and then go on to an evening of social or community activity. Lumping together the condition of being "unable to move around freely" with being "unable to attend to his personal requirements" seems, to an active, self-reliant person confined to a wheelchair, mistaken and unfair. A person with insufficient muscular function to push himself in his wheelchair does need to travel with someone to help him. Most disabled people going on vacation are as likely as anyone else to prefer traveling with a friend for companionship, but that's a far cry from having a white-coated "attendant" on duty. And, just like his able-bodied colleagues, a handicapped business traveler is most likely to be traveling alone.

Many organizations of the handicapped feel so strongly about a third restriction imposed by the airlines that they have organized "wheel-ins" on airport tarmacs to dramatize the situation. This restriction involves the quota applied to the number of wheelchair passengers that can be carried on any given flight. Frequently the limit is four or five.

"Suppose I want to go to a convention with five friends," says one woman, "and we're all in wheelchairs. Why should we have to split up? It would be inconvenient, time consuming, and an infringement on our rights."

All of those things may be true, but in this case the carriers have to cope with some very real problems involving personnel, equipment, and evacuation procedures. By law, they are required to have one flight attendant for every fifty passenger seats. The attendants are responsible for prompt evacuation of passengers in case of emergency. This means that each attendant is responsible for the evacuation of fifty passengers. The number of emergency exits on an aircraft varies with the type of plane. Thus, the possibility that a flight might carry more incapacitated passengers than there were flight attendants or exits has led to restrictions on the number of wheelchair passengers allowed on an airplane.

"If anything happens, I'll just go down with everyone else," is a frequently voiced statement among the handicapped, but, as the Association of Flight Attendants reminded the FAA in a letter concerning safety procedures, "Even if the handicapped person is willing to assume the risk to his own person . . . it must be remembered that the risk is not his alone to assume." There is the possibility of an immobile person's blocking the evacuation of other passengers or of occupying a flight attendant's sole attention to the detriment of other passengers.

Lest the quota system still appear to be overly discriminatory toward handicapped passengers, it must be emphasized that it is observed flexibly and pragmatically by many carriers. For example, there have been many charter flights consisting entirely of wheelchair-bound passengers, and it is likely that there will be many more in the future because international activity among organizations of the handicapped is very much on the increase. As far back as 1968, El Al carried a full planeload of paraplegics to the Wheelchair Olympics in Israel, although a spokesman for the airline confessed, "The passengers were fine, but we were nervous every minute of the way." The Eastern Paralyzed Veterans Association has been flying its wheelchair basketball teams and its track and field teams to tournaments all over the United States and Europe since the end of World War II. Each year international events such as the Olympiad for the Physically Disabled and the Stoke-Mandeville Games as well as regional meets for handicapped athletes attract groups traveling with their wheelchairs.

According to Dr. Ludwig G. Lederer, a leading authority on aerospace medicine and former corporate medical director of American Airlines, the airlines fly hundreds of handicapped people on scheduled and charter flights every year and try to accommodate them with a minimum of special arrangements. "Most handicapped persons have an unusually high degree of self-reliance," Dr. Lederer says. "They want to be able to travel as freely as anyone else, and in most cases they are perfectly capable of doing so. The airlines' job is simply to look out for their safety."

Like many other segments of the American population, the handicapped have stopped nursing their grievances. They have become vocal and militant. And they have had some effect. In 1977, the FAA issued a series of amendments to the Federal Aviation Regulations in order to supply guidelines for the airlines to observe in providing safe carriage "of persons who may require the assistance of another person during an emergency evacuation." These amendments didn't come out of a clear blue sky. First the FAA issued a preliminary notice of the rules it was proposing and solicited public comment on them. Then the FAA Civil Aeromedical Institute (CAMI) conducted simulated air carrier aircraft evacuations using individuals with actual handicaps, both alone and in groups including persons without handicaps. It also examined air carrier accident files to find out if any evacuation problems had been attributed to the presence of handicapped people on board.

CAMI got a lot of comments. On the chief proposal, which included the requirement of having a physician's statement and restrictions on the number of handicapped persons per flight, 90 percent of the responses were negative. In its evacuation research, the institute found a "lack of evidence of significant delays created by handicapped persons in actual aircraft evacuations." CAMI, in its simulated tests, discovered that "many non-ambulatory handicapped persons reached the exit with remarkable speed using seat backs for support or in the sitting position, pulling themselves backwards with their arms."

As a result, the amendments were revised. The most significant regulation provides that "a passenger may not be refused transportation on the basis that his transportation would or might be inimical to safety of flight unless the certificate holder [airline] has established procedures (including reasonable notice requirements) for the carriage of passengers who may need the assistance of another person to move expeditiously to an exit in the event of an emergency."

The key phrase in that sentence is "established procedures." By May 16, 1977, every American carrier had to submit to the FAA its own policy regarding transportation of the handicapped, taking into consideration type of aircraft used, seating configurations, passenger loading facilities, and other aspects of the carrier's operating environment. The FAA has the power to direct changes in procedures if needed "in the interest of safety or in the public interest." In order to help the airlines formulate a rational, fair policy toward carriage of handicapped people, the FAA issued an advisory circular containing guidelines for establishing procedures.

Once an airline had established its procedures, it could not refuse to carry a handicapped person *unless* (1) the passenger failed to comply with the notice requirements in the certificate holder's procedures; or (2) the passenger could not be carried in accordance with the certificate holder's procedures. If this sounds as though you're back to square one, you would be right, except that at this point the Civil Aeronautics Board (CAB), once the powerful regulator of the conditions under which the airlines were allowed to do business, got into the act. After deregulation of U.S. airlines mandated the termination of the CAB, the board in its sunset days issued a set of detailed regulations governing treatment of handicapped passengers. These established a general policy requiring carriers to ensure that handicapped passengers receive "reasonable access" to air transportation and that carriers cannot discriminate against any qualified handicapped person.

A "qualified" handicapped person is one who tenders payment for air travel, whose carriage will not jeopardize the safety of the flight or the health of other persons, and who is "willing and able to comply with reasonable requests of airlines personnel." Airlines are prohibited from providing "separate or different" services to qualified handicapped persons unless such actions are "reasonably necessary" or requested by the handicapped traveler.

The CAB also issued a set of more detailed rules governing the carriage of handicapped passengers that originally were binding only on commuter or regional airlines receiving some form of direct federal support. The nonsubsidized major airlines were expected to regard these deatailed rules only as guidelines.

The specific rules require that the deaf and blind be given "timely access" to schedules and flight information and that dog guides be allowed on all domestic flights as well as on international flights provided their carriage is consistent with the laws of the foreign country involved. Such personal equipment as crutches, canes, and wheelchairs must be allowed to the extent permitted by FAA safety regulations.

Carriers cannot require attendants for handicapped travelers unless the passenger needs "extraordinary personal care," such as feeding, assistance in the lavatory, or nursing services. Each carrier, furthermore, must designate a particular employee to make determinations on the need for an attendant. Carriers are required to make available such services as medical oxygen for on-board use, wheelchairs, ramps, and mechanical lifts for boarding and deplaning. They are permitted to impose "reasonable, non-discriminatory charges" for their use.

With the demise of the CAB, the Department of Transportation (DOT) took over many of its functions. Soon after, the United States Court of Appeals, responding to a suit brought by the Paralyzed Veterans of America and other groups representing the disabled, ruled that all airlines should observe the tighter rules outlined governing carriage of handicapped passengers. This would have been good news, except that the Justice Department then petitioned the Supreme Court to reverse this ruling and apply the stricter rules only to the smaller lines receiving direct federal subsidies. The issue is still undecided.

Foreign flag carriers are not required to comply with any of these rules or guidelines. In practice, most do adhere to them fairly closely, and some travelers think that foreign flag carriers are actually more accommodating, more likely to bend rules, and not as wary of lawsuits as the American lines. But if a handicapped traveler thinks he has been treated unfairly by a foreign carrier, he has no recourse except a stiff letter to the president of the company.

## CURRENT POLICIES OF
## MAJOR DOMESTIC AND FOREIGN AIRLINES

Keep in mind that the data in the charts on pp. 12–23 are subject to change and that nothing should be taken for granted. As a rule, airlines that permit dog guides do not charge to transport them, except in the case of New York Helicopters, which requires a half-fare ticket for the dog because of the limited space on a helicopter. For flights to destinations outside the mainland of the United States, please see pp. 31–34 for information about quarantine, inoculations, and acceptability of transient dogs. If a charge for using a carrier's oxygen is not indicated, it is supplied free, although this, like everything else, should be checked when making travel arrangements.

## THE ACCESSIBLE AIRPLANE

United Airlines, which in 1947 became the first carrier to accept non-ambulatory passengers and their wheelchairs, in 1982 took delivery of a fleet of Boeing 767s specially configured for wheelchair accessibility. Designed as a cooperative effort by Boeing, United, and rehabilitation experts, the 767 features a lavatory that is accessible by using the on-board aisle wheelchair. The lavatory has an oversize door, low-entry threshold, built-in assist devices, a lowered door latch, lever handles for toilets and doors, and increased floor space. Most important is a ten-foot-square privacy area adjacent to the lavatory for extra maneuvering room or to accommodate a companion of a dependent passenger. The airplane also has four seats (two in first class and two in coach) with movable arm rests for easier transfer between aisle chair and passenger seat.

According to the Boeing Commercial Airplane Company, the following airlines have also purchased 767s: Air Canada, Air New Zealand, All Nippon, American, Ansett, Avianca, Braathens, Britannia, CAAC (People's Republic of China), China Air, Delta, Egyptair, El Al, Ethiopian, Japan Air Lines, Kuwait Airways, Pacific Western, Qantas, Trans Brazil, and TWA. However, configuration is up to the individual airline, so they may not all take advantage of the lavatory maneuvering area, aisle chair, or special seat provisions. When making a reservation, it pays to inquire whether the airline flies 767s on the desired route and if special interior accommodations are available.

Air Canada has purchased new wheelchairs that not only allow mobility for disabled passengers in airport terminals but also adapt to allow passengers to go directly to their seats on all aircraft types—without the need to change to a different wheelchair. Provisions for the special transportation of wheelchairs have been introduced, and new wheelchair-accessible washrooms are available on the airline's B-767 aircraft. Other innovations include the in-flight video safety demonstrations, which feature closed-captioned instructions for the hearing impaired.

Ansett Airlines of Australia, with North American headquarters in Los Angeles, has instituted a service called An-

## POLICIES OF MAJOR AIRLINES REGARDING TRANSPORTATION OF THE HANDICAPPED

| | Aisle chair for boarding | Medical Certification | Quota for wheelchairs |
|---|---|---|---|
| Aerolineas Argentinas | Yes | Yes | No |
| Aer Lingus | Yes | No | No |
| Air Canada | Yes; need 24 hours' notice | Depends on nature of handicap | Yes, but flexible |
| Air France | Yes | Depends on nature of handicap | Depends on route and aircraft; special arrangements for groups |
| Air India | Yes | In case of serious illness | One each in First and Executive Class; three in Economy Class |
| Air New Zealand | Yes, on 72 hours' notice | Yes | No |
| Alaska Airlines | Yes | Health certificate required if under physician's care | No |
| Alitalia | Yes | No | Yes |
| Aloha Airlines | Yes, on two hours' notice | Only for mental patients | 18 on one flight; with advance notice, may be waived for groups |
| American Airlines | Yes | Under certain conditions | Limited by aircraft type; exceptions by advance arrangement |
| Austrian Airlines | Yes | In most cases | No |
| Braniff | Yes | No | No |

| Companion required | Seeing guide dogs | Hearing guide dogs | Oxygen carriage requirements |
|---|---|---|---|
| Yes | Yes | Query airline | Query airline |
| No | No dogs from United States to British Isles or other prohibiting area | Same | Query airline |
| 50% fare reduction for companion (only if one is needed) | Yes | Yes | Within Canada: 48 hours' notice; international, 72 hours; must use carrier's oxygen; $40 minimum charge |
| Only if not self-sufficient | Two per cabin, leashed and muzzled | Same* | Query airline; escort required |
| Depends on nature of handicap | Yes | Yes | Query airline |
| In some cases | No | No | One weeks' notice; $50 fee; medical certification |
| If not self-sufficient and flight is over two hours | Yes | Yes | Must give 24 hours' notice and use carrier's oxygen equipment |
| Only if not self-sufficient | Yes | Yes | Query airline |
| Only for mental patients | Yes | Yes | Advance notice; must use carrier's oxygen equipment |
| For stretcher patients and blind/deaf who cannot read Braille | Yes | Yes | Must use carrier's oxygen by advance reservation and with medical approval; fee |
| If requested by Austrian Airlines Medical Service | Yes | Yes | Query airline |
| Yes | Yes | Yes | Query airline |

*Deaf passengers accompanied by dogs must have a certificate attesting to deafness or a FREMEC.

**POLICIES OF MAJOR AIRLINES REGARDING TRANSPORTATION OF THE HANDICAPPED (continued)**

| | Aisle chair for boarding | Medical Certification | Quota for wheelchairs |
|---|---|---|---|
| British Airways | Yes | At discretion of carrier | No; special arrangements for groups |
| British Caledonian | Yes | Only in case of recent surgery or hospital treatment | 20 per flight |
| CAAC (People's Republic of China) | Request when making reservation | Yes | Depends on aircraft |
| Canadian Pacific | Yes | Only for medical cases | Restricted by Canadian government according to aircraft and degree of disability |
| Cathay Pacific | Yes | Only for mental impairment or serious illness | Only for quadriplegics, depending on aircraft |
| Delta Air Lines | Yes | Only if passenger is seriously ill, has just been released from hospital, requires oxygen, or under similar circumstances | No |
| Eastern | Yes | If passenger is unaccompanied, non-ambulatory | Depends on aircraft |

| Companion required | Seeing guide dogs | Hearing guide dogs | Oxygen carriage requirements |
|---|---|---|---|
| Only if not self-sufficient | No dogs from United States to British Isles or other prohibiting area | Same | 48 hours' notice; must use carrier's oxygen. Passenger's own cylinders can be filled at London only. No charge. |
| No | Only United Kingdom internal flights | Same | Query airline |
| Yes, unless medical certificate says not necessary | Yes | Yes | Query airline |
| Only if not self-sufficient or a large number of wheelchair passengers are on board* | Yes | Yes | Sufficient advance notice to place oxygen pack at boarding station. Medical clearance from passenger's physician required. No charge, but policy subject to change. |
| Only if not self-sufficient | Must be crated and carried in cargo | Same | 24 hours' notice; must use carrier's oxygen unless advance permission obtained to use own |
| Only if not self-sufficient | Yes | Yes | Must use carrier's oxygen at $40 per bottle; advance notice required |
| Only if not self-sufficient | Yes | Yes | 48 hours' notice for oxygen required during flight; must use carrier's oxygen. Passenger's own oxygen unit accepted only as checked baggage if cylinder is empty and properly packaged. |

*Passengers who require a companion are charged 50 percent of the applicable fare when traveling domestically within Canada. Proof of need for companion is required.

**POLICIES OF MAJOR AIRLINES REGARDING TRANSPORTATION OF THE HANDICAPPED (continued)**

| | Aisle chair for boarding | Medical Certification | Quota for wheelchairs |
|---|---|---|---|
| El Al | Only at Kennedy Airport, New York | No | No |
| Finnair | Yes | Yes, according to IATA resolutions and recommended practices | No; group arrangements must be made in advance |
| Frontier | Yes | No | No; group arrangements must be made in advance |
| Iberia | Yes | Only for passengers with special needs | No |
| Icelandair | No | Only for medical cases | 10; special arrangements for groups |
| Japan Air Lines | Yes | Yes | Only for battery-powered chairs |
| KLM | Yes | Yes | No |
| Korean Air Lines | Yes | No | No |
| Lufthansa | No | Only in certain cases* | Depends on aircraft and type of disability |

*FREMEC accepted.

| Companion required | Seeing guide dogs | Hearing guide dogs | Oxygen carriage requirements |
|---|---|---|---|
| Only if not self-sufficient | Yes | Yes | Must use carrier's oxygen as determined by El Al's physician and passenger's physician; $75 fee. |
| Depends on nature of handicap | Yes | Yes | First-aid equipment and oxygen system required by flight-safety regulations. No other types accepted. |
| No | Yes | Yes | Per FAA regulations; query airline |
| Only if not self-sufficient | Yes; one per cabin, up to three per plane | Same | Medical certificate and companion required |
| No | Yes, but not to Iceland | Same | Must use carrier's oxygen; three days' notice required |
| No | One per flight; 72 hours' notice | Same | Must use carrier's oxygen; 72 hours' notice; medical certificate required |
| No | Yes | Yes | Query airline |
| No | Yes | Yes | Query airline |
| Only for groups exceeding quota and for passengers requiring medical certification | Yes, muzzled | Same | With advance notice, carrier can supply for 150 minutes to 11 hours of constant use. Carrier's oxygen equipment must be used. No respirators permitted on board. |

**POLICIES OF MAJOR AIRLINES REGARDING TRANSPORTATION OF THE HANDICAPPED (continued)**

| | Aisle chair for boarding | Medical Certification | Quota for wheelchairs |
|---|---|---|---|
| New York Helicopters | No. Passengers must be able to board and de-plane unas-sisted. Wheelchairs can be stowed in baggage bin. | No | One per flight |
| Northwest Orient | Yes | For some categories; call in advance | Four to 10, depending on aircraft |
| Ozark Air Lines | Yes | No | No |
| Pan Am | Yes | For special cases | Two to five severely handicapped (does not include self-sufficient paraplegics or the blind with dog or companion) |
| Piedmont | Yes | Only when person does not meet usual accep-tance guidelines | No |
| Qantas | Yes | No, but medical report desirable for briefing air-port staff and cabin crew | 12 on Kangaroo Route, 10 on Pacific routes |
| Regent Air | No | Depends on disability | No |

| Companion required | Seeing guide dogs | Hearing guide dogs | Oxygen carriage requirements |
|---|---|---|---|
| No | Yes, with advance arrangement and purchase of half-fare ticket for dog | Same | Will carry passenger's oxygen |
| For some categories; call in advance | Yes | Yes | Must use carrier's oxygen; 24 hours' notice; physician's statement and Liability Release Statement required |
| Only if mentally disturbed or not self-sufficient | Yes | Yes | Must use carrier's equipment |
| Only if not self-sufficient | Yes | Yes | Must use carrier's oxygen; physician's certificate required; $40 fee. |
| Only if not self-sufficient | Yes | Yes | Continuous in-flight medical oxygen is available to passengers with prescriptions from their physicians at a charge of $40 per one-way trip. Passenger's oxygen is not permitted in cabin and may not be checked as baggage unless fully discharged. |
| Depends on itinerary and degree of disability | No | No | Must use carrier's oxygen; 48 hours' notice; fee. Passenger's oxygen can be carried as excess baggage (for a fee) if packed according to safety regulations. |
| Only if non-ambulatory | Yes | Yes | Cannot accept passengers requiring oxygen in-flight |

**POLICIES OF MAJOR AIRLINES REGARDING TRANSPORTATION OF THE HANDICAPPED (continued)**

| | Aisle chair for boarding | Medical Certification | Quota for wheelchairs |
|---|---|---|---|
| Republic | Yes; request when making reservation | Only for sedation, heart condition, or respiratory ailment | Yes |
| Sabena | Yes | If currently, or have recently been, medically ill | No |
| SAS | Yes | For those who require medical attention during flight and/or individual attention enplaning, deplaning, or during flight | No |
| Singapore Airlines | Yes | Yes | 10 on B-747 |
| South African Airways | No | Yes | Three to 10, depending on aircraft and number of crew |
| Swissair | Yes | Depends on nature of disability | Four to eight; special arrangements for groups |
| TAP Air Portugal | No | Medical cases only | Yes |
| Thai Airways International | No | Yes | No, but contingent upon total passenger load |
| Transamerica | Yes | Only if not self-sufficient of if serious heart condition exists | No |

| Companion required | Seeing guide dogs | Hearing guide dogs | Oxygen carriage requirements |
|---|---|---|---|
| If unable to move from cabin seat to rest room | Yes | Yes | Must use carrier's oxygen; 48 hours' notice; $40 fee. Physician's statement indicating maximum air flow per hour required. |
| No | Yes | Yes | Query airline |
| If not self-sufficient or must be lifted, moved, or supported during flight | Yes | Yes | Must use carrier's oxygen; advance notice |
| One for every five handicapped persons traveling together | Only in First Class, one per flight | No | Query airline |
| Only if not self-sufficient | Yes | Yes | Order when making reservation. No charge |
| Only in some cases | Yes | Yes | Passenger's equipment accepted subject to inspection at check-in. Airline must be notified when making reservation. |
| Medical cases only | Yes | Yes | Must use carrier's oxygen; no charge |
| If assistance required to use lavatory or to provide medication, or if oxygen is needed | Yes | Yes | Carrier will supply. Own may be carried with prior approval. |
| If passenger requires care in-flight or affects safety of other passengers | Yes | Yes | Query airline |

**POLICIES OF MAJOR AIRLINES REGARDING TRANSPORTATION OF THE HANDICAPPED (continued)**

| | Aisle chair for boarding | Medical Certification | Quota for wheelchairs |
|---|---|---|---|
| TWA | Yes | At discretion of airline; may be required for trips over eight hours | Three to 10 unaccompanied; no limit accompanied |
| United Airlines | Yes | For therapeutic oxygen | For unaccompanied, non-ambulatory passengers |
| USAir | No | Only for pregnancies in ninth month | One to four unaccompanied, non-ambulatory |
| UTA French airlines | Yes | Yes | Yes |
| Varig | Yes | Not unless medical attention required | Advance notice for more than two per flight |
| Western | Yes | May be required for quadriplegics | No |

| Companion required | Seeing guide dogs | Hearing guide dogs | Oxygen carriage requirements |
|---|---|---|---|
| Depends on disability | Yes | Yes | Must use carrier's oxygen; fee based on amount used and number of flight coupons |
| In some cases | Yes | Yes | Must use carrier's oxygen; 72 hours' notice for Medical Department clearance; service charge of $40 per flight coupon |
| Only if not self-sufficient | Yes | Yes | Constant oxygen not permitted |
| Stretcher cases only | Yes, leashed and muzzled | Same | Must use carrier's oxygen; charge according to amount used. Medical certificate stating quantity, duration, and intervals required one week before departure. |
| Only if not self-sufficient | Only in baggage compartment | Same | Available upon request for intermittent use. Passenger's oxygen carried in baggage compartment in accordance with FAA regulations. |
| Quadriplegics only | Yes | Yes | Must use carrier's oxygen; $40 fee per flight segment |

sacare that records details related to permanent and semipermanent disabilities in its computerized reservations system, eliminating the need for a medical clearance each time a disabled person travels. Additional services to the handicapped include an all-weather system for transporting wheelchair-bound or infirm passengers into the aircraft; a unit that lifts up to fourteen disabled people at a time; direct-dial reservations units for deaf passengers; and movable armrests on its Boeing 727s and 737s.

British Airways, which handles about 150 wheelchair passengers daily at London's Heathrow Airport, is putting a newly designed 15-inch skychair aboard all 747 and TriStar aircraft. It will allow disabled passengers to move about the cabin or to go to the lavatory unassisted.

Other airlines offer some special features on a smaller scale. Eastern's B-727s have some seats with folding armrests, and all seats on A-300s and B-757s have them; the B-757 has an assist rail in one coach lavatory. Frontier, which has lifted all restrictions on handicapped passengers (except for not seating them in exit rows), provides special evacuation information to blind and non-ambulatory passengers. This line does not consider blind and/or deaf passengers as being handicapped. Its flight attendants are trained in body mechanics and lifting and carrying procedures developed at Denver's Craig Hospital, an international center for treatment of spinal cord injuries. Both Piedmont and Japan Air Lines use the "Manten Chair," manufactured in Japan, which can be adapted for ground and on-board use, eliminating the need to transfer a non-ambulatory passenger from one chair to another when making flight connections. Piedmont has fold-up armrests on two aisle seats of nearly all aircraft for ease of transfer from aisle chairs to passenger seats.

In May 1985, World Airways became the first U.S. airline

to offer a comprehensive program of "total access" for disabled passengers. As part of the new program, World's entire fleet of DC-10s has been equipped with collapsible on-board aisle wheelchairs, seats with movable armrests, lavatories with "grab bars," in-flight briefing books printed in Braille, and captioned in-flight briefing videotapes for the deaf and hearing impaired. All World personnel have gone through in-depth training sessions to sensitize them to the special needs of elderly and handicapped travelers. In addition, the airline has established toll-free numbers for disabled passengers. By voice: (800) 526-9287; in California, (800) 772-3550. By telecommunications devices for the deaf: (800) 621-4337; in California, (800) 223-7287.

## MAKING RESERVATIONS

Airlines are just like everyone else—they hate surprises. Do them and yourself a favor by not showing up at the airport in your wheelchair ten minutes before departure of a flight on which you have no reservation. A miracle may happen and you may be able to get on the plane, but it's more likely that you won't. It's also likely that there will be a lot of ill-feeling between you and the airline personnel (remember, they hate surprises) that could have been avoided if you had gone about things in the right way.

The right way means *give the airlines plenty of notice* and *be honest.* Make your reservations as early as possible. When you talk to a reservations agent, explain precisely what your condition is and what you can and cannot do. If you are using the services of a travel agent, do the same with him or her. If you use oxygen, a respirator or any mechanical device, you must say so. (A remarkable number of people show up unexpectedly at airports lugging their own oxygen—which isn't permitted—or expecting to plug in a respirator on an airplane.) If you cannot get out of your wheelchair, make sure it's understood that "just a few steps" might as well be Mount Everest as far as you are concerned.

Joni Eareckson, a quadriplegic who travels frequently in the course of her public-relations work, comments: "I work with a travel agency and I always remind the agents to make sure that the airline with whom I'm dealing understands my situation. Whenever I've had problems at an airline terminal, it's because they didn't understand that I couldn't get *out* of my wheelchair."

If you find you're not getting specific answers to your questions, ask to talk to a supervisor. Get the names of the people you talk to. Get written confirmations of everything they tell you. The usual procedure is to have the fact that you are in a wheelchair, plus any other pertinent information, fed into a computer. You will be told almost instantly if a particular flight is not available because its quota of wheelchair passengers has already been filled. (This may be philosophically distasteful, but it really doesn't happen very often.) The earlier you make your reservation, the more likely it is that you will have no trouble getting the flight you want. When you call Lufthansa and mention that you are making a reservation for a handicapped person, you will immediately be switched to a special reservations agent who knows what's what.

A travel agent can be your best friend if you make sure he understands clearly and precisely what your needs are. If you are absolutely honest with him, you will benefit from using his services because he can take many details off your hands and it will not cost you anything extra. But whether you deal with an agent or directly with an airline, ask questions and keep reconfirming your reservations. You are not being a pest. You are a paying passenger. As a British Airways reservations agent told a woman in a wheelchair who was worried about being a problem, "Madam, we don't have any problem passengers."

## GETTING TO THE AIRPORT

Allow plenty of time. Plan to be *at the airport* no later than *one hour before departure on domestic flights, two hours on overseas flights.* It isn't fair to yourself or to the airline to show up at the last minute, because then you won't get the kind of service you are entitled to. By allowing sufficient time, you will have first boarding on the plane and be assured a good seat. Even if your seat reservation is already in the computer, you have to be there early enough to be boarded ahead of the other passengers. Make use of curbside check-in, if available, for your luggage. Usually you can be taken as far as the plane in your own wheelchair (sometimes right on board in it).

Travel agents can find a list of bus and limousine services that provide transportation for the handicapped to major airports in the United States in the North American edition of the *OAG Travel Planner.* It also includes car-rental services for the handicapped and a listing of tour operators with programs for handicapped travelers. When making the reservation, be sure to explain exactly what the traveler's needs are and find out if they can be accommodated. Equipment and company policies are subject to frequent change.

If you would like to drive your hand-controlled car to New York's John F. Kennedy International Airport or LaGuardia Airport, but are reluctant to leave it in a parking lot while you are away, you might like to use the services of Auto Baby

Sitters. This company, patronized by over 200,000 travelers a year, picks your car up at the airport, stores it in its indoor, fireproof, secure headquarters and then delivers it back to the airport in time for your arrival. It has the same pickup and delivery service for hotels and piers. The cost is less than long-term parking at an airport or a municipal garage and safety and security are incomparably better. The drivers are accustomed to hand-controlled cars. For a brochure explaining how the system works, write to Auto Baby Sitters, 827 Sterling Place, P.O. Box 285, Brooklyn, New York 11216. Telephone (718) 493-9800.

## BOARDING THE PLANE

Look on this as an experience fraught with adventure, excitement, and drama. And it helps to have a sense of humor. With big airports and big airplanes, there are seldom any problems. Usually you can be wheeled to the door of the plane in your own chair along the jetway or boarding sleeve that everyone uses. On jumbo jets, such as the Boeing 747, the DC-10, and the L-1011, the widest wheelchair can go through the entrance and directly to your seat in the front row. With some configurations, the chair can even go down the aisle to any seat, although it is better to have a reserved front-row seat on the aisle.

It gets more complicated with smaller planes and smaller airports. Most airlines can provide a boarding chair, which is a very narrow, high-backed chair especially constructed to go through the entrance and down the aisle of planes smaller than the jumbos. (The passenger is strapped into it.) If there is no jetway, you may be pushed up a ramp in the boarding chair, carried up a flight of steps, or lifted on a forklift. There is also a new type of boarding chair that has a climbing mechanism, so that with two assistants the wheelchair itself actually climbs the steps.

Patty Hughes, wife of a television executive, reports: "When I landed in London, there was no sleeve, so they carried me down the steps and at the foot of the steps had a van with a hydraulic lift waiting with the door open, picked me up, and swooped me over to the terminal. Marvelous!"

TWA has developed a vehicle called a Handicapped Lift for use in terminals that do not have jetways. It's an enclosed, elevator-type unit that can handle two wheelchairs and an operator at a time, eliminating the need for carrying the handicapped or injured passengers up and down outdoor stairs. This should be a blessing all around since many airlines are reluctant to allow their personnel to carry passengers bodily; at the same time, many handicapped people dislike being carried because they feel uncomfortable or unsafe.

Be sure to make it clear that you will need your own chair as soon as you arrive at your destination. You can get an "escort ticket" that says you need to have the wheelchair available as soon as you deplane. It should be folded and placed in the baggage compartment so that it will be readily available upon landing. Many airlines will place your wheelchair in the baggage compartment last so that it will be the first item unloaded. Some airlines recommend that you purchase a bicycle container (usually about $3) at the airport to protect the chair.

## BATTERY-OPERATED WHEELCHAIRS

It is advisable to avoid traveling with battery-operated wheelchairs. As Joni Eareckson explains: "I don't use the battery-operated chair when I travel. It doesn't fold conveniently and it's very heavy. It would also be dangerous to take it on too many airplanes because it's a fine piece of equipment. It would get knocked around in baggage compartments. I think it's advisable for anybody who travels to use a push chair. Battery-operated chairs are very valuable to those of us who use them and it would be a catastrophe to have one damaged in transit."

However, if it is absolutely necessary to travel with a battery-operated wheelchair, new FAA regulations provide:

1. Wheelchairs with *nonspillable* batteries may be carried as checked baggage if the battery is disconnected, the terminals are insulated to prevent short circuits, and the battery is securely attached to the wheelchair.
2. Wheelchairs with *spillable* batteries may be carried as checked baggage if the chair can be loaded, stored, secured, and unloaded always in an *upright position*. The battery must be disconnected, the terminals insulated to prevent short circuits and the battery securely attached to the wheelchair.

Otherwise, a spillable battery must be removed from the chair and properly packed for storage according to FAA regulations.

These rules bring U.S. airlines into conformity with international civil air practice, so that once a battery-operated wheelchair has been accepted by a carrier in accordance with the preceding conditions, it may be transported by air anywhere in the world that these conditions can be met. Passengers or travel agents are responsible for giving the airlines correct information about wheelchairs and batteries when making reservations.

## OXYGEN

Carriage of oxygen on aircraft is also subject to FAA regulations concerning hazardous materials. If you have a battery-powered respirator, you must advise the airline ahead of time and they may supply oxygen for you, at a charge. However, airlines are not required to do so. You may bring your own oxygen into the cabin only if it has been supplied by a firm, such as Air Medic, that packs it according to FAA specifications. However, you must get clearance from the airline ahead of time. The FAA advises using the airline's oxygen and shipping your own—which has been purchased from an oxygen supply company and is properly pressurized, packed, and labeled—as cargo, if your airline permits.

## BLINDNESS AND DEAFNESS

Blind travelers present so few problems to the airlines that they are not really considered handicapped. On domestic flights a blind person may sit wherever he likes with his dog curled up at his feet. A window seat is often preferred so that seatmates will not have to step over the dog, and a bulkhead seat gives the dog more room to stretch out. Sticks can now be stowed at seats. Flight attendants are instructed to tell a blind passenger when the seat belt and smoking signs go on and off and to point out the positions and functions of the various buttons on the armrest. If a blind person is traveling alone, the attendant will be glad to describe the food and how it is arranged on the tray.

The late Roy Andries de Groot, the wine and food expert, who was a great international traveler, took his smoky brown German shepherd, Automne, with him everyplace she was permitted to go. He had to leave her, with great regret, in the Netherlands when he visited Great Britain. When asked if he thought he might be able to get a dog on loan in Britain, he pooh-poohed the idea, saying, "Using a loan dog would be like borrowing a wife." Most dog guides are, in fact, female, which enabled de Groot to perform a clever feat of animal training. "You can't explain to a dog that you're going to be in a holding pattern for two hours," he said, "and she wants her walk on schedule, so I trained one dog, Nusta, to sit on a toilet seat on a plane!"

While you may safely assume that dog guides are carried in the passenger compartment of any airline not specifically listed as prohibiting them, always check to be absolutely sure. The airlines are not against dogs or blind people. Rather, whether a dog may be carried or not depends almost entirely on the destination. A number of island-countries and one island-state are rabies-free and are convinced that they can stay that way by imposing strict quarantine on imported animals. The usual quarantine period is 120 to 180 days and the animal must have been shipped in the baggage compartment. Thus, it would be impossible for a blind tourist to have the use of his dog. Destinations imposing this restriction are Australia, Hawaii, Hong Kong, Ireland, New Zealand, and the United Kingdom. But when planning a trip to any foreign country other than Canada, contact the embassy or nearest consular service of that country to find out what the regulations are. Canada admits dog guides without requiring medical certification.

Bermuda requires a permit to bring in a dog guide. It can be obtained by writing to the Department of Agriculture, P.O. Box 834, Hamilton 5, Bermuda. Regulations are as follows: All animals entering Bermuda must be accompanied by a veterinarian's certificate certifying freedom from all types of infectious and contagious diseases; it must also certify that the animal has not been infected by, or exposed to, rabies and has not been in a rabies area during the previous six months. Animals from countries other than Great Britain, Australia, New Zealand, or Jamaica must also have a certificate stating that they have been vaccinated against rabies not less than one month nor more than one year immediately prior to arrival in Bermuda.

Sweden and Norway, which require a 120-day quarantine for pets, make exceptions for dog guides. However, the dog has to be examined at the airport by a veterinarian and could be rejected or put under quarantine. Norway requires a rabies certificate and advises prospective visitors who wish to bring a dog guide to write well in advance to the Ministry of Agriculture–Norwegian Veterinary Directorate, Oslo, Norway. Denmark imposes no quarantine but requires a rabies certificate.

Everyone understands the problems of the blind and tries to be helpful, but few people realize that the deaf are in many ways far more handicapped and far more likely to be treated with callousness or indifference. A deaf person cannot hear that his flight is ready for departure; that it has been delayed or cancelled; that the bar is open; or that meal service has been delayed because of turbulence. He or she cannot hear the instructions for evacuation or the pilot's reassurance that "we're just going through a little rough weather, folks."

Flight attendants are now instructed to point out written safety and evacuation procedures to deaf people individually. A travel agent can be of particular help to a deaf traveler by making sure that the airline knows his condition and understands his needs. He needs someone to speak up for him in every sense because, without any identifying sign, such as a dog or a cane, he can so easily be overlooked. As a matter of fact, there is a movement to train hearing dog guides and a number of them are in use. The American Humane Society sponsors a program—begun in 1973 by the Humane Society of Minnesota—to train hearing dog guides. These dogs, most of them taken from pounds, go through a 20-week program that trains them to respond to certain words, noises, and situations and to attract their masters' attention physically.

United Airlines offers a special reservations service (limited to the continental United States) for those who have a hearing or speech impairment. Flight reservations, hotel accommodations, and car rentals may be obtained by calling toll-free: (800) 323-0170 (in Illinois the number is [800] 942-8819). The phone links a typewriter-style machine (TTY) in the prospective passenger's home or office with a similar machine in United's reservations office. Prospective passengers can communicate with a specially trained reservations agent twenty-four hours a day. A similar service is offered by World Airways. The toll-free number is (800) 621-4337; in California it's (800) 223-7287.

## SPECIAL FOOD REQUIREMENTS

Back in the mists of airline history, someone asked for kosher food, someone else was a vegetarian, and the next thing anyone knew, the airlines were offering, among them, more than thirty types of special menus catering to various medical, religious, and cultural needs. These include such genuine esoterica as gastrectomy, hypoglycemic, and gluten-free menus. (A gastrectomy, in case you didn't know, is the surgical removal of all or part of the stomach. Such a passenger can have in-flight repasts of poached and soft-boiled eggs and mashed and baked potatoes, all laced with butter, salt, and sugar and served at frequent intervals.)

## SPECIAL MENUS AVAILABLE ON AIRLINES

| Menu<br><br>*Based on medical needs:* | Aerolineas Argentinas | Aer Lingus | Air Canada[1] | Air France | Air India | Air New Zealand | Alaska Airlines | Alitalia | American Airlines[4] | Austrian Airlines |
|---|---|---|---|---|---|---|---|---|---|---|
| Bland | • | • | | | • | • | • | • | • | |
| Bland/Meat-Free | • | • | | | • | • | | • | | |
| Bland/Ulcer | • | • | | | • | • | | • | | |
| Diabetic | • | • | • | • | • | • | • | • | • | • |
| Dietetic | • | • | | • | • | • | • | • | | |
| Fat-Free | • | • | | | • | • | | • | | |
| Gastrectomy | • | • | | | | • | | • | | |
| Gluten-Free | • | • | • | | • | • | | • | | |
| High Calorie/ High Vitamin | • | • | | | • | • | | • | | |
| High Protein | • | • | | | • | • | | • | | |
| High Protein/Low Fat | • | • | | | • | • | | • | | |
| Hypoglycemic | • | • | | | • | • | | • | | |
| Lactose-Restricted | • | • | | | • | • | | • | | |
| Low Calorie | • | • | • | | • | • | • | • | • | |
| Low Calorie/ Low Cholesterol | • | • | | | • | • | • | • | | |
| Low Calorie/ No salt added | • | • | | | • | • | | • | | |

| Menu<br><br>*Based on medical needs:* | Aerolineas Argentinas | Aer Lingus | Air Canada[1] | Air France | Air India | Air New Zealand | Alaska Airlines | Alitalia | American Airlines[4] | Austrian Airlines |
|---|---|---|---|---|---|---|---|---|---|---|
| Low Carbohydrate | • | • | | • | • | • | | • | • | |
| Low Cholesterol | • | • | • | | • | • | • | • | • | |
| Low Fat | • | • | • | • | • | • | | • | | |
| Low Residue | • | • | | | • | • | | • | | |
| Low Sodium | • | • | | | • | • | • | • | • | • |
| Non-Residue | • | • | | | • | • | | • | | |
| Salt-free | • | • | • | • | • | • | • | • | | |
| Vegetarian | • | • | • | • | •[2] | • | • | • | • | • |
| Vegetarian (Lacto-Ovo) | • | • | • | | | • | • | • | • | |
| Weight-Watchers | • | • | | | • | • | | • | | |
| *Based on other than medical needs:* | | | | | | | | | | |
| Hindu | • | • | • | • | •[2] | • | | • | • | |
| Kosher | • | • | • | • | • | • | • | • | •[5] | • |
| Kosher (Salt-free) | • | • | | • | • | • | • | • | | |
| Mormon | • | • | • | | | • | | • | | |
| Moslem | • | • | | • | • | •[2] | | • | • | • |
| Oriental | • | • | | • | | • | | • | | |
| Soul | • | • | | | | • | | • | | |

| Menu / Based on medical needs: | Braniff | British Airways | British Caledonian | CAAC[6] | Canadian Pacific[7,8] | Cathay Pacific[1] | Delta | Eastern | El Al[11,12] | Finnair |
|---|---|---|---|---|---|---|---|---|---|---|
| Bland | | • | • | • | • | | •[9] | • | • | • |
| Bland/Meat-Free | | • | • | • | | | | | | • |
| Bland/Ulcer | | • | | • | | • | | • | | • |
| Diabetic | | • | • | • | • | • | | • | • | • |
| Dietetic | | • | • | • | • | • | | | | • |
| Fat-Free | | • | • | • | | | | | • | • |
| Gastrectomy | | • | | • | | • | | | | |
| Gluten-Free | | • | • | • | • | • | | • | • | • |
| High Calorie/ High Vitamin | | • | | • | | | | | | • |
| High Protein | | • | • | • | | | | | | • |
| High Protein/Low Fat | | • | • | • | | | | | | • |
| Hypoglycemic | | • | • | • | • | | | • | | • |
| Lactose-Restricted | | • | • | • | | | | • | | • |
| Low Calorie | | • | • | • | • | • | •[9] | • | • | • |
| Low Calorie/ Low Cholesterol | | • | • | • | | • | | | • | • |
| Low Calorie/ No salt added | | • | • | • | | • | | | | • |

| Menu<br><br>Based on<br>medical needs: | Braniff | British Airways | British Caledonian | CAAC[6] | Canadian Pacific[7,8] | Cathay Pacific[1] | Delta[1] | Eastern | El Al[11,12] | Finnair |
|---|---|---|---|---|---|---|---|---|---|---|
| Low Carbohydrate | | • | • | • | | | | • | | • |
| Low Cholesterol | | • | • | • | • | • | •[9] | • | • | • |
| Low Fat | | • | • | • | | | •[9] | • | | • |
| Low Residue | | • | | • | | | | | | |
| Low Sodium | | • | • | • | • | | •[9] | • | • | • |
| Non-Residue | | • | | • | | | | | | |
| Salt-free | | • | • | • | | • | | | • | • |
| Vegetarian | | • | • | • | • | • | •[9] | • | • | • |
| Vegetarian (Lacto-Ovo) | | • | • | • | • | • | •[9] | | | • |
| Weight-Watchers | | | • | • | | | | | | |
| *Based on other than medical needs:* | | | | | | | | | | |
| Hindu | | • | • | • | • | • | | | | • |
| Kosher | • | • | • | • | • | • | •[10] | • | • | • |
| Kosher (Salt-free) | | | • | • | | | | | | • |
| Mormon | | | | • | | | | | | |
| Moslem | | • | • | • | • | • | •[9] | | | • |
| Oriental | | • | • | • | | • | | | | |
| Soul | | | | • | | | | | | |

| Menu<br><br>*Based on medical needs:* | Frontier[5] | Iberia | Icelandair[1] | Japan Air Lines[13,14] | KLM | Korean Air Lines | Lufthansa[1] | Northwest Orient[1,16,17,18] | Ozark Air Lines[15] | Pan Am[1] |
|---|---|---|---|---|---|---|---|---|---|---|
| Bland | | • | • | | • | • | • | • | | • |
| Bland/Meat-Free | | • | • | | • | • | • | • | | |
| Bland/Ulcer | | • | • | • | • | • | • | | | |
| Diabetic | • | • | • | • | • | • | • | • | | |
| Dietetic | • | • | • | • | | • | • | | • | |
| Fat-Free | | • | • | • | • | • | • | | | |
| Gastrectomy | | • | | | • | • | • | | | |
| Gluten-Free | | • | • | | • | • | • | • | | • |
| High Calorie/<br>High Vitamin | | • | | | | • | | | | |
| High Protein | • | • | | | | • | | | | • |
| High Protein/Low Fat | | • | | | • | • | | | • | |
| Hypoglycemic | | • | • | | | | • | | | |
| Lactose-Restricted | | • | | | • | • | • | • | • | |
| Low Calorie | | • | • | • | • | • | • | • | • | • |
| Low Calorie/<br>Low Cholesterol | | • | • | • | | • | • | | • | |
| Low Calorie/<br>No salt added | | • | • | | • | • | • | | | |

| Menu<br><br>*Based on medical needs:* | Frontier[5] | Iberia | Icelandair[1] | Japan Air Lines[13,14] | KLM | Korean Air Lines | Lufthansa[1] | Northwest Orient[1,16,17,18] | Ozark Air Lines[15] | Pan Am[1] |
|---|---|---|---|---|---|---|---|---|---|---|
| Low Carbohydrate | | • | • | | | • | • | | • | |
| Low Cholesterol | • | • | • | • | • | • | • | • | • | • |
| Low Fat | • | • | • | • | • | • | • | | • | • |
| Low Residue | | • | | • | • | • | • | | | |
| Low Sodium | • | • | • | | | • | • | • | | • |
| Non-Residue | | • | | | | • | | | | |
| Salt-free | | • | • | • | • | • | • | • | | |
| Vegetarian | • | • | • | • | • | • | • | • | | • |
| Vegetarian (Lacto-Ovo) | • | • | | • | | • | • | • | • | |
| Weight-Watchers | | • | • | | • | • | | | | |
| *Based on other than medical needs:* | | | | | | | | | | |
| Hindu | | • | | • | • | • | • | • | | • |
| Kosher | • | • | • | • | • | • | • | • | • | • |
| Kosher (Salt-free) | | • | • | | • | | • | | | |
| Mormon | | • | | | • | | | | | |
| Moslem | | • | • | • | • | • | • | • | | • |
| Oriental | | • | | | • | • | • | • | | |
| Soul | | • | | | | | | | | |

| Menu<br><br>*Based on medical needs:* | Piedmont[16,19] | Qantas | Regent Air[3,6] | Republic[1,8] | Sabena | SAS | Singapore | South African Airways | Swissair | TAP Air Portugal |
|---|---|---|---|---|---|---|---|---|---|---|
| Bland | ● | ● | ● | | ● | | ● | | ● | ● |
| Bland/Meat-Free | | ● | ● | | ● | | ● | ● | ● | ● |
| Bland/Ulcer | | ● | ● | | ● | | ● | | ● | ● |
| Diabetic | ● | ● | ● | ● | ● | ● | ● | ● | ● | ● |
| Dietetic | ● | ● | ● | ● | ● | | ● | ● | ● | ● |
| Fat-Free | | ● | ● | | ● | ● | ● | ● | ● | ● |
| Gastrectomy | | ● | ● | | ● | | ● | | | |
| Gluten-Free | ● | ● | ● | | ● | | ● | ● | ● | ● |
| High Calorie/ High Vitamin | | ● | ● | | ● | | ● | | ● | ● |
| High Protein | ● | ● | ● | | ● | | ● | | ● | ● |
| High Protein/Low Fat | | ● | ● | | ● | | ● | ● | ● | ● |
| Hypoglycemic | | ● | ● | | ● | | ● | | ● | ● |
| Lactose-Restricted | | ● | ● | | ● | | ● | | ● | ● |
| Low Calorie | ● | ● | ● | ● | ● | ● | ● | | ● | ● |
| Low Calorie/ Low Cholesterol | ● | ● | ● | ● | ● | ● | ● | ● | ● | ● |
| Low Calorie/ No salt added | | ● | ● | | ● | | ● | ● | ● | ● |

| Menu<br><br>*Based on medical needs:* | Piedmont[16,19] | Qantas | Regent Air[3,6] | Republic[1,8] | Sabena | SAS | Singapore | South African Airways | Swissair | TAP Air Portugal |
|---|---|---|---|---|---|---|---|---|---|---|
| Low Carbohydrate | • | • | • |  | • |  | • |  | • | • |
| Low Cholesterol |  | • | • |  | • | • | • | • | • | • |
| Low Fat | • | • | • |  | • | • | • | • | • | • |
| Low Residue | • | • |  |  | • |  | • |  |  | • |
| Low Sodium | • | • | • | • | • |  | • | • | • | • |
| Non-Residue |  | • |  |  | • |  | • |  |  | • |
| Salt-free |  | • | • |  | • | • | • | • | • | • |
| Vegetarian | • | • | • | • | • | • | • | • | • | • |
| Vegetarian (Lacto-Ovo) | • | • |  |  | • |  | • | • | • | • |
| Weight-Watchers |  | • | • |  | • |  | • |  |  | •[20] |
| *Based on other than medical needs:* |  |  |  |  |  |  |  |  |  |  |
| Hindu | • | • |  |  | • | • | • | • | • | • |
| Kosher | • | • | • | • | • | • | • | • | • | •[3] |
| Kosher (Salt-free) |  | • | • |  | • |  | • | • | • | •[3] |
| Mormon |  | • |  |  | • |  | • |  |  | •[3] |
| Moslem | • | • |  |  | • | • | • | • | • | •[3] |
| Oriental | • | • |  |  | • | • | • | • | • | •[3] |
| Soul |  |  |  |  | • |  |  |  |  |  |

| Menu<br><br>Based on<br>medical needs: | Thai Airways[3,4,6] | Transamerica | TWA | United Airlines[1,8] | USAir[8,21] | UTA | Varig | Western[3] | | |
|---|---|---|---|---|---|---|---|---|---|---|
| Bland | • | • | | • | | | • | • | | |
| Bland/Meat-Free | • | • | | | | | • | • | | |
| Bland/Ulcer | • | • | | | | | • | • | | |
| Diabetic | • | • | • | • | • | • | • | • | | |
| Dietetic | • | • | | | | • | • | • | | |
| Fat-Free | • | • | | | | | • | • | | |
| Gastrectomy | | • | | | | | • | • | | |
| Gluten-Free | | • | | | | | • | • | | |
| High Calorie/<br>  High Vitamin | | • | | | | | • | • | | |
| High Protein | • | • | | | | | • | • | | |
| High Protein/Low Fat | • | • | | | | | • | • | | |
| Hypoglycemic | • | • | | | | | • | • | | |
| Lactose-Restricted | • | • | | | | | • | • | | |
| Low Calorie | • | • | • | • | • | | • | • | | |
| Low Calorie/<br>  Low Cholesterol | • | • | • | | | | • | • | | |
| Low Calorie/<br>  No salt added | • | • | | | | | • | • | | |

| Menu<br><br>Based on medical needs: | Thai Airways[3,4,6] | Transamerica | TWA | United Airlines[1,8] | USAir[9,21] | UTA | Varig | Western[3] | | |
|---|---|---|---|---|---|---|---|---|---|---|
| Low Carbohydrate | • | • | • | • | | | • | • | | |
| Low Cholesterol | • | • | | • | • | | • | • | | |
| Low Fat | • | • | | • | • | | • | • | | |
| Low Residue | • | • | | | | | • | • | | |
| Low Sodium | • | • | • | • | • | | • | • | | |
| Non-Residue | | • | | | | | • | • | | |
| Salt-free | • | • | | | | • | • | • | | |
| Vegetarian | • | • | • | • | • | • | • | • | | |
| Vegetarian (Lacto-Ovo) | • | • | | | | | • | • | | |
| Weight-Watchers | | • | | | | | • | • | | |
| **Based on other than medical needs:** | | | | | | | | | | |
| Hindu | • | • | • | | | • | • | • | | |
| Kosher | • | • | • | • | • | • | • | • | | |
| Kosher (Salt-free) | • | • | | | | | • | • | | |
| Mormon | | • | | | | | • | • | | |
| Moslem | • | • | • | | | • | • | • | | |
| Oriental | • | • | | | | | • | • | | |
| Soul | | • | | | | | • | • | | |

[1] Also fish, seafood, or fruit plate
[2] No advance notice necessary
[3] 48 hours' notice
[4] 6 hours' notice, except as indicated
[5] 3 hours' notice
[6] 72 hours' notice
[7] Also Feingold diet
[8] Also children's menus
[9] 3 hours' notice
[10] 8 hours' notice
[11] All meals are kosher
[12] Also available: soft diet, dairy, natural, baby meal, sick-baby meal, glatt kosher and any other religious requirement
[13] 10 hours' notice
[14] Medical meals not indicated available on 72 hours' notice
[15] Must be requested by 6:00 P.M. the day prior to flight
[16] Also fruit plate or snack
[17] 6 hours' notice
[18] Also Rajneesh
[19] Also oral liquid
[20] 36 hours' notice
[21] Must be requested by 8:00 P.M. the day prior to flight

If you are on a special diet, always ask the airline if it can accommodate you. It's unlikely that you're the only person in the world with those special needs. If your specific diet is not available, the airline will tell you what would be closest to it so that you can select the foods you are permitted to have. The best time to order a special meal is when you make your reservation for a flight. Lead time necessary to board these meals varies considerably from one carrier to another and from one menu to another. Special requests at some stations may require up to seventy-two hours' notice. Usually twenty-four hours are sufficient to be sure of getting what you want; exceptions are noted on the following charts. Remember that availability of special menus is subject to change.

## AIRPORTS

Traditionally airports were not designed—they just grew as the air travel industry grew, with the result that even able-bodied people have found them inconvenient, uncomfortable, and confusing. Even many of the newer ones, designed according to rational plans, became obsolete as soon as they were finished. As a result, airports have been in an almost constant state of construction and reconstruction, a situation that allows great opportunity for creating a more accessible environment for the handicapped. In the United States, federal funding is almost always necessary to assist airport construction, and thus, as a result of recent legislation, barrier-free facilities are mandatory. In other countries there is also a growing awareness of accessibility needs, and airports are gradually being brought up to more acceptable standards.

One of the most useful new aids to the traveling public is a booklet called *Access Travel: Airports*—the result of a survey of over 550 major air terminals worldwide conducted by the Airport Operators Council International. The information, which is in chart form, is valuable to all sorts of people, not only those in wheelchairs but also elderly people, families with small children—anybody who has difficulty moving around easily. Specific information is given about the accessibility of parking, exterior and interior circulation, arrival and departure, elevators, ramps, stairs, doors, boarding, telephones, rest rooms, eating and drinking facilities, and many other features that are of vital interest to those who need them but that have often been overlooked in the past by airport designers.

For single, free copies of *Access Travel: Airports*, write to Access America, Washington, D.C. 20202 or Consumer Information Center, Pueblo, Colorado 81009 (ask for Item No. 632K).

Corporate travel planners, travel agents and other members of the travel industry can find the same information in a constantly updated form in the *OAG Travel Planner and Hotel/Motel Guide*. Published as an adjunct to the *Official Airline Guides*, it is geared for travel industry personnel and frequent business travelers rather than for the general public. North American, European, and Pacific Area editions are available. They include hotel listings for almost 30,000 properties; those with special handicapped rooms are indicated by a + symbol. Single copies are $25; a one-year subscription (four issues) is $70.

As a result of an advisory from the Airport Operators Council International, most airports now permit hearing dog guides on their premises and many of them have installed telephone amplifiers that permit some deaf people to use telephones.

At National Airport in Washington, D.C., a specially equipped courtesy van is available for use by handicapped travelers for transportation to any point in the airport between 6:00 A.M. and 11:00 P.M. There is no charge and the van may be reserved outside these hours by prearrangement. Call (703) 892-2750 or use direct-line telephones located near the USAir baggage-claim area, the North Terminal exit, and the Commuter Terminal lobby exit. The service may also be arranged through your airline or by a Skycap.

## AIRPORT GUIDEBOOKS FOR THE HANDICAPPED

London, England: *Who Looks After You at Heathrow Airport? (Gatwick Airport, Stansted Airport).* Separate guides to London's three airports. Available free from British Airports Authority, 2 Buckingham Gate, London SW 1, England.

New York, New York: *Facilities and Services for the Disabled* (covers LaGuardia, Newark International, and Kennedy International airports). Available free from The Port Authority of New York and New Jersey, Aviation Public Services Division, One World Trade Center, Room 65N, New York, New York 10048.

Norfolk, Virginia: Ask for the brochure on facilities for the handicapped. Available free from Information & Services Department, Norfolk Port Authority, Norfolk International Airport, Norfolk, Virginia 23518.

Paris, France: *Aéroport Charles de Gaulle* and *Aéroport d'Orly.* General information in French and English (not specifically for the handicapped) about the Paris airports, including layout of passenger terminal, access, facilities available, and useful hints. Order from Aéroports de Paris, Suite 2551, One World

Trade Center, New York, New York 10048. Telephone: (212) 432-1093.

At least seventy other airports around the world offer some sort of brochure outlining their facilities for the handicapped. Write to the information services department of the airport at your departure and destination cities.

## USEFUL PUBLICATIONS CONCERNING TRANSPORTATION OF THE HANDICAPPED

*Air Transportation of Handicapped Persons,* AC No. 120-32. Identifies problems facing handicapped air travelers and provides guidelines for developing airline policies to help alleviate them. Valuable for travel industry personnel. Available free of charge from the Department of Transportation, Distribution Unit, TAD-443.1, Washington, D.C. 20590.

*Coping with Inaccessibility: Assisting the Wheelchair User.* A practical book with step-by-step procedures for handling each situation illustrated. Both architectural and transportation barriers are covered. Available for $6 (prepayment required) from Rehabilitation Research and Training Center, The George Washington University, Ross Hall, Room 714, 2300 Eye Street, N.W., Washington, D.C. 20037.

*Customs Hints for the International Traveler.* Available on a cassette. Order free from Mary Stim, the Public Services Division, U.S. Customs Service, Washington, D.C. 20229, or telephone (202) 566-8195. Also free from the same source but in print only: *The Travel Pack*, which contains seven to ten brochures with helpful information for the international traveler.

*Disabled Passengers Air Travel Guide.* Information for passengers flying Qantas, the Australian airline, much of which is applicable to other airlines as well. Available free by calling Qantas toll-free reservations numbers: in California, (800) 622-0850; Alaska and Hawaii, (800) 227-3000; elsewhere in the United States, (800) 227-4500.

*Incapacitated Passengers Air Travel Guide.* The most detailed information available about traveling by air with any sort of temporary or permanent disability. Details airline and airport procedures and facilities; explains various effects of flying on the human body and how to adjust to them; offers sound, practical advice to the prospective traveler. Order by sending U.S.-dollar check or money order for $4 per copy, made payable to "International Air Transport Association," to Publications Agent, IATA, 2000 Peel Street, Montreal, Quebec, Canada H3A 2R4. (Cost to IATA member airlines and travel agents in North, Central, and South America is U.S. $2 per copy.)

*Incapacitated Passengers Handling Guide.* Similar to the above, but oriented to airline personnel and travel agents. Order as for above. Cost to IATA member airlines and travel agents in North, Central, and South America is U.S. $1.50 per copy for up to one hundred copies.

*Incapacitated Passengers Physicians Guide.* Another version of the same booklet, this one for nonairline physicians who may have to clear incapacitated and handicapped people for air travel. Order as above. Cost to IATA member airlines and travel agents in North, Central, and South America is U.S. $1.50 per copy.

*Seeing Eye Dogs as Air Travelers.* Intended for airline personnel but useful for anyone who wants to learn about blind travelers and their dog guides. Available from The Seeing Eye, Inc., Morristown, New Jersey 07960.

*Travel for the Patient with Chronic Obstructive Pulmonary Disease.* Tips for air travel by people with emphysema, chronic bronchitis, and other respiratory problems. Available for $2 (prepayment required) from Harold M. Silver, M.D., P.C., 1601 Eighteenth Street, N.W., Washington, D.C. 20009.

*Travel Primer for the Sick and Handicapped.* Depressing title, but useful information in a simply written little pamphlet focusing on preparation for air travel and inflight situations. Free from any Swissair office or by mail from Swissair, P.O. Box 845, Radio City Station, New York, New York 10102.

Finally, if you find flying a thrill, not a hassle, and would like to be in the pilot's seat yourself, being wheelchair-bound need not stop you. There is a portable hand control with which a paraplegic can fly the Piper Cherokee 140 without using the feet. It is fully FAA certified and available from the manufacturer, Arnold R. Allen, 2252 Barbara Drive, Clearwater, Florida 33546.

# 2

# BUSES, TRAINS, AND SHIPS

## BUSES

Bus travel for the handicapped took a giant leap forward when Greyhound Lines hired Joni Eareckson, a quadriplegic, as spokesman for its Helping Hand Service. Joni, paralyzed from the shoulders down in a diving accident shortly after graduating from high school in 1967, is bright, articulate, and attractive. She is also a seasoned traveler who has covered many miles by bus and plane to spread the word that handicapped people have the same interests and aspirations as everyone else and do not want to be isolated from the mainstream of society.

"I hate to think of myself as handicapped," Joni says. "I like to think of myself as normal except I can't get up steps easily. I want to make the public more empathetic—not sympathetic, but understanding."

Joni has since gone on to careers as an artist (she uses a special holder to grip drawing tools between her teeth) and a popular lecturer to college and church groups. Greyhound, a pioneering company in making travel accessible and affordable for people with limited mobility, has continued to facilitate travel for the handicapped.

Helping Hand service is a plan that allows a handicapped person and a companion to travel together on a single ticket. The object of the program is for the companion to provide assistance to the handicapped person during boarding and exiting and with any needs en route. The only requirements are that the pair travel together for the complete trip and that the companion be capable of rendering all necessary assistance.

In actual practice, Greyhound employees usually are cheerfully willing to assist the companion with boarding and exiting, especially if the handicapped passenger needs to be carried bodily to the seat. And such assistance will be necessary if the passenger cannot get out of his or her chair. There are two reasons for this: first, a wheelchair cannot make the turn from the entrance of a bus to the aisle; second, the aisles are only 14 inches wide and there is no narrow boarding chair of the sort that airlines use. As a handicapped passenger, however, you and your companion will always be given "first-on" seating on trips originating in your home city, and Greyhound will try to set aside *both* front seats for your comfort (unless you prefer to sit in the smoking section in the rear). On buses originating in other cities, you will have first-on seating after through passengers have returned to their seats, and the front seats will be yours if they are not already occupied.

New Greyhound terminals, as well as old ones being remodeled, are designed with the handicapped in mind and include such features as wide doorways, accessible rest rooms and food service areas, lowered telephones and water fountains, and ramps and handrails, where necessary. But bear in mind that there are hundreds of terminals, and it will be a long time before all of them can meet even minimum standards of accessibility.

To qualify for this two-for-the-price-of-one program, the handicapped person must present a written statement from a doctor stating that he or she needs a companion for physical assistance in bus travel. Here is a sample of the statement required, to be written on the physician's letterhead:

### CERTIFICATE OF ELIGIBILITY

Greyhound Lines, Inc., allows an attendant to travel with a disabled person when the person is disabled to the extent of requiring the assistance of an attendant to board, alight, and travel on a bus.

(Name)_____

is disabled and in my judgment can travel by bus if accompanied by an attendant to assist him or her in boarding, alighting, and traveling on a bus.

The disability is _____permanent _____temporary

Date_____

Doctor's name_____

Address_____

(Signature of doctor)_____

The medical certificate requirement is not intended to make the handicapped person feel like a second-class traveler. Rather, it is a necessary precaution against the human urge to commit larceny—there actually have been cases of people attempting to pose as handicapped in order to get the special fare!

Since 1980, Greyhound has been reaching out to deaf and other communicatively handicapped people with its Silent Information Service. Utilizing telecommunications devices for the deaf (TDD/TTY units), the communicatively handicapped can have toll-free access from anywhere in the United States to Greyhound's telephone information center in Allentown, Pennsylvania. Operators are prepared, day and night, to provide information on bus schedules, fares, package express rates, and baggage. Handicapped people who own or have access to a TDD/TTY unit of any manufacture can call (800) 345-3109 (in Pennsylvania [800] 322-9537) for fast, accurate information about Greyhound's entire route system.

Helping Hand Service applies not only to all Greyhound regular rates but also to such special fares as the Ameripass, which is good for unlimited travel all over the United States and Canada via the routes of Greyhound Lines and certain other carriers. The Ameripass also includes special discounts on hotels, meals and sightseeing. Nonmotorized folding wheelchairs, crutches, walkers, and similar devices are carried free in the baggage compartment and do not count as part of the allowance of pieces of luggage for each person.

Two free brochures, *A Traveler's Guide for the Handicapped* and *Greyhound's Silent Information Service*, may be ordered by writing to Public Relations, Greyhound Lines, Inc., 1810 Greyhound Tower, Phoenix, Arizona 85077.

Trailways, Inc., is just as interested as Greyhound in encouraging bus travel by handicapped people. Trailways offers a plan that allows any handicapped person, including the blind, to take alone a companion-helper on any of its regularly scheduled routes at no extra charge. (The plan is not available for tours.) Each person is allowed 150 pounds of luggage or three suitcases, and wheelchairs are carried free and do not count as luggage. According to Robert Buschner, vice-president for marketing, "Our Eagle Model 10 motorcoaches are unique in that they can transport any kind of wheelchair, whether motorized or manual."

Trailways also requires a physician's letter attesting to the need for a companion. The company will reserve a front seat for you and its employees will carry you to it, if necessary.

Trailways is following recommended guidelines for the handicapped in building new terminals and remodeling old ones. There are lowered telephones, sill-less doors, and rest rooms with extra-wide stalls. But again, there are hundreds of terminals and it may be several years before they all meet accessibility standards. New terminals have been built in New York City, El Paso, Denver, San Antonio, Albuquerque, Fort Worth, Houston, and Boston, and a new facility is planned for Washington, D.C.

For more information about the services Trailways offers, write to Roger Rydell, Trailways, Inc., 1500 Jackson Street, Suite 410, Dallas, Texas 75201.

Neither of these cross-country bus lines sets any sort of quota on the number of wheelchair passengers carried. Both do ask that you call the terminal in advance of your departure to let the line know that you are using the special service. Tell the line when you intend to arrive at the terminal and which bus you are going to take. Plan your trip in advance and read the schedules carefully. By careful planning you may be able to avoid changing buses or having to transfer to another terminal. If such transfers are unavoidable, inform the Trailways customer service agent or Greyhound terminal information clerk about what kind of assistance you may need.

Try to travel midweek, when crowds are smaller. You will get better service and be more comfortable. If you would like to break your trip with an overnight stop, both Trailways and Greyhound can make arrangements for you at a comfortable hotel convenient to the terminal. Be sure to specify your accessibility needs.

When it comes to sightseeing tours and short trips by bus, handicapped travelers may encounter more difficulties than on long-distance trips with the major nationwide carriers, which, as we have discussed, make a special effort to accommodate them.

Chartering a bus for a handicapped group presents equipment problems in some places. Bob Eichel, of the National Paraplegia Foundation, says "I've tried to organize one-day or weekend tours for the handicapped within a radius of 250 miles of New York City. But I've never been able to find a coach in this city that has a lift for the handicapped. I once went on a charter trip with Greyhound and the driver had to lift everyone in and out of the bus. That was really too much. Then there are many people who would like to go on trips to Boston and Washington, but they want to stay in their wheelchairs on the bus, so you have to have the seats removed, and I couldn't get that."

## AMERICAN RAILWAYS

If there is anything good to be said for the decline of American railroads over the past twenty or thirty years, it is that all the equipment was in such bad shape when Amtrak took over that it was necessary to begin with massive replacement of rolling stock. Almost all of the old, "conventional" cars have been replaced by new equipment designed with handicapped passengers very much in mind. A major part of the new stock consists of Amfleet cars that replace many of the old coaches. Amfleet is the starting point for Amtrak's new design approach, and its special features were adopted after consultation with organizations of the handicapped.

In the food service car on Amfleet trains, a special seat with a folding armrest allows a handicapped person to transfer easily out of and into his or her wheelchair. No passenger is allowed to occupy a wheelchair on these trains. All special facilities for the handicapped are confined to the food-service car. There is no restriction on the number of handicapped people that can travel in standard train seats, but only one special seat is available and that is the one in the food-service car. If a train is made up with two food-service cars, there will be two such seats available.

The reason for putting the special seat in the food-service car is that it is impossible to move a wheelchair through a train. Thus, the special toilet for the handicapped is in the food-service car. It is big enough for a wheelchair to enter and is equipped with handrails. The entrances to all Amfleet cars are wide enough for a wheelchair to go through, but from that point the passenger is usually transferred from the wheelchair to a seat on the train. All Amfleet cars have plenty of room at each end to store a wheelchair, but in the case of a group of wheelchair passengers traveling together there might be a problem, since these short-distance trains do not always have a baggage car. Check with Amtrak when making reservations for a group with several wheelchairs.

As far as wheelchairs are concerned, Amtrak assumes no liability for luggage or other property (including wheelchairs) carried on board the train in the passenger compartments. The liability for property checked in the baggage car is $500 per person. Battery-operated wheelchairs may be taken on the train and stored behind the special handicapped seat. However, if the chair is more than forty-three inches deep, it will stick out into the aisle and interfere with the movement of other passengers.

One important point to remember is that in the Northeast corridor (Boston–New York–Washington) there is no reserved seating except on premium-fare Metroliners or on Club Car (first class) sections of other trains. The handicapped seat cannot be reserved either—you must simply get on the train and hope for the best. But while the special seat is a convenience, the most important thing is to be in the food-service car, where special facilities are available. You must, however, be able to transfer to a regular seat with a minimum amount of help from Amtrak employees. While it is unfortunate that it's all very much of a gamble, the likelihood that any one train would have two people who both need the special chair is very small. If you are planning to go on a non-reservation train, call the station a day or two before traveling and speak to the station manager. (At a major terminal, like Penn Station in New York, only a couple of hours' notice is necessary.) Tell the station manager your needs and he will make arrangements to make it easier for you, not only at your station of departure, but also at your destination. Redcap service, available at all the large stations and at many of the smaller ones, is free to Amtrak passengers (though tips are sometimes offered and gratefully received). The station manager will make sure you have a Redcap to meet you.

In New York state only, Amtrak has another kind of new equipment called the Turboliner. It also has facilities designed for the handicapped, but they differ somewhat from those on Amfleet. The special handicapped seat is in the Custom Class section. There is a handicapped rest room that is large enough for a person in a wheelchair to enter, and it is fitted with grab bars. The special seat with a fold-down armrest is similar to the one on Amfleet. Again, there is only one such seat to a car, and no one can stay in a wheelchair on the trip. The entrances to the cars are wide enough for wheelchairs to go through. The food-service car is one car removed, but conductors and trainmen can be asked to remind the food-service attendant that there is a handicapped person who needs to be served at his or her seat. A pull-down table allows for eating in comfort. The usual $5 charge for riding in Custom Class is waived for the handicapped.

The jazziest new Amtrak equipment consists of bilevel cars arranged in several different double-decker configurations. These are long-distance trains with many amenities, including a ramp entryway. There is a double-decker sleeping car that has a special room for the handicapped with an upper and lower bed. The upper bed, obviously, would be used by an able-bodied traveling companion. This is a real room, so large that it goes across the entire width of the railroad car. It is at the end of the car on the lower level, with windows on both sides, and it's most attractive. The room is so spacious that you could remain in your wheelchair if you wanted to, although Amtrak strongly advises that you transfer to a seat because it is safer.

Most of these long-distance trains have at least two sleeping cars, so there will be at least two special compartments available. (They can be released for general sale if no handicapped people reserve them.) The handicapped bedroom is priced like a regular first class bedroom because it has toilet facilities in the room. But there are also coach arrangements for the handicapped. Entrance to bilevel coach cars is by ramp in the center of the car, so that a wheelchair can roll right in. Every coach car has a handicapped seat and rest room, which, of course, are on the lower level.

Since there is no way for a wheelchair to go from car to car, all food and beverage services are taken care of by an attendant. The cars are very well set up for such service, and all the coach seats are equipped with tray tables. In these cars the special seat is a little bit different from those on the Amfleet and Custom Class cars. It is a swivel seat that can be swung out to face the aisle, but it does not have a folding armrest.

On long-distance trains it is necessary to make reservations in advance, and the handicapped should reserve as much in advance as possible. Always outline your needs fully to the passenger agent. If Amtrak cannot accommodate you, it will tell you so, but you can be assured that the line will make every effort possible to enable you to travel and to do so comfortably.

But the biggest barrier to train travel is the situation in the terminals. They are almost impossible! Amtrak knows about this situation and is trying to change it as old stations are renovated and new ones built. It is attempting to make renovated stations barrier-free, but the renovations aren't always economically or architecturally feasible. All new stations have been built for barrier-free access, but many of the old ones have stairs to the train platforms, low platforms that make it necessary to walk up steps to the train, and inadequate toilet facilities.

In the Northeast corridor, all trains come in level with the platform and employees can help a passenger bridge the small gap between train and platform. However, no employee is allowed to lift a person in a wheelchair up and down steps, whether in the terminal or from a low platform to a train. Employees can push passengers in wheelchairs and assist them in and out of their seats. There are no portable ramps.

A bright note is the new rail passenger station in Miami, Florida, which was designed to make rail travel more convenient and attractive for handicapped and elderly passengers. Ramps, an elevator, accessible rest rooms, and telephones have been incorporated into the barrier-free structure.

BLINDNESS
Amtrak's toll-free reservations numbers operate twenty-four hours a day, seven days a week, so a blind person can call anytime for information about trains, schedules, fares, etc.

Dog guides are permitted in passenger compartments (no other dogs are). Reduced rates—25 percent off regular fares one-way or round trip—are available to the blind and other handicapped travelers, but there is no discount for a wheelchair attendant. On all new trains, station stops are announced over a public address system.

## DEAFNESS
Amtrak has a special reservations system for deaf passengers. It works through two special teletypewriters that can communicate with an estimated ten thousand deaf people who have similar teletypewriters in their homes. Many institutions make such teletype equipment available to any deaf person who needs to use it. In Amtrak's case, the deaf person dials a special toll-free number, then puts his telephone into a holder that connects it with the teletypewriter at Amtrak's central reservations bureau. He can get information, make reservations, whatever he wants through this system. The Amtrak agent types responses to all questions, which are then transmitted to the deaf person's teletypewriter. The nationwide toll-free numbers to Amtrak's teletypewriter are (800) 523-6590 and (800) 523-6591. Residents of Pennsylvania call (800) 562-6960. On board a train, a deaf person should make his condition known to the conductor, who will then be careful to alert him to station stops.

## AMTRAK'S NATIONWIDE RESERVATION NETWORK
Amtrak provides a toll-free number ([800] USA RAIL; in Pennsylvania, [800] 562-6960) in each of the forty-eight contiguous states for reservations and information. Avoid calling at the very busiest hours—from 9:00 A.M. to 1:00 P.M. and from 5:00 P.M. to 9:00 P.M. The best times to call are very early in the morning, midafternoon, or late at night.

Amtrak reservationists are on duty twenty-four hours a day. Almost all travel agencies are Amtrak-accredited and can use their own limited-access telephone lines to Amtrak to get information and make reservations.

Write for the free booklet *Access Amtrak: A Guide to Amtrak Services for Elderly and Handicapped Passengers* to Amtrak Distribution Center, P.O. Box 7717, Itasca, Illinois 60143.

## EUROPEAN RAILWAYS

There is a fine network of railroads in Europe, and many European countries have equipment and stations that are accessible to the handicapped. However, information is difficult to come by and information in English is almost non-existent. Unless you or your travel agent have contacts in Europe who could check out accessibility and make arrangements on the spot, seeing Europe by train remains a dim possibility for most handicapped American travelers.

### BRITAIN
British Rail has embarked on an ambitious program to make its new equipment accessible. The latest type of first-class Inter City coach has wide entrance doors and a removable seat in the area nearest the toilet, so a wheelchair can be rolled in and the passenger can remain in it for the trip. There is no extra charge for a wheelchair passenger holding a second-class ticket. These coaches operate on long-distance runs in England and Wales. Stations, too, are being renovated with accessibility in mind.

Railway stations in Britain remain a serious problem, since most of them were built many years ago, when little thought was given to the traveling requirements of the handicapped.

But remarkable improvements are under way, including curb cuts, handrails, clearer signing and white lining of danger points, induction loops for hearing-aid wearers, portable ramps, and more toilets for the disabled. Interest and good will abound, so if you would like to travel by train in Britain, write well in advance to the Area Manager, British Rail, at your departure station, and every effort will be made to take care of you. In the words of a company spokesman, "British Rail is anxious to provide as comfortable a journey as possible for the disabled passenger and would therefore be grateful to receive early prior advice of travel." An informative little booklet called *British Rail and Disabled Travelers* is free from BritRail International Inc., 630 Third Avenue, New York, New York 10017; telephone (212) 682-5150.

## GERMANY

If you can read German, you're in luck. Otherwise, you had better forget about train travel in Germany unless you will be accompanied by a German-speaking friend. GermanRail publishes a fifty-page brochure that contains explicit information for handicapped travelers. Available only in German, its title is *Reiseführer für unsere behinderten Fahrgäste* (Travel Guide for Handicapped Passengers). It lists accessibility information about more than four hundred stations in West Germany. For a small fee, GermanRail can arrange door-to-door baggage transportation, even to and from places that do not have railway stations. The booklet is available at no charge from GermanRail, 747 Third Avenue, New York, New York 10017. Handicapped travelers or their travel agents interested in further information should contact the nearest GermanRail office. There are offices in New York, Boston, Chicago, Denver, Houston, Los Angeles, San Francisco, and Toronto.

## FRANCE

A booklet called *Supplément au Guide Pratique du Voyageur: à l'intention des personnes à mobilité réduite* (Supplement to the Traveler's Practical Guide: For the Use of Handicapped People) provides information for the handicapped on how to make train reservations, which trains are specially equipped, and what facilities exist in various railroad stations in France. Published by French National Railroads (SNCF), the booklet is in French and available only in France. For a visitor to France, the most important things to know are that reservations should be made well in advance (they can be made up to six months in advance by mail) and that there are specially equipped trains on some runs called *trains aménagés*, which, in both first and second class, have seats reserved for handicapped people. A traveler wanting to remain in his wheelchair can reserve a space in the first-class coach for the cost of a second-class ticket. Reservations for *trains aménagés* should be made no later than forty-eight hours before the date of departure. At the major railway stations, reception services staffs (recognizable by their orange-trimmed uniforms) are available to give assistance to handicapped passengers.

For further information, contact the office of the French National Railroads nearest you. The North American headquarters is at 610 Fifth Avenue, New York, New York 10020. Other offices are in Beverly Hills, Chicago, Coral Gables, Montreal, San Francisco, and Vancouver.


## SHIPS

There are no regularly scheduled transatlantic liners anymore and few passenger ships anywhere that merely transport you to a destination. Ship travel today means cruising. That's something that ought to be more popular with handicapped people than it is, but two obstacles stand in the way—mental blocks and architectural blocks. Many handicapped people say: "I've never dreamed of going on a ship. It just never entered my mind." But on second thought it always seems to intrigue them.

The architectural blocks stem from the nature of ships, which are built to keep out water and have little room to spare. At every doorway there's a sill sticking up that effectively keeps out water and wheelchairs. Bathroom entrances have them too, and bathrooms are usually minute and crammed with plumbing fixtures at odd angles. Doorways on most ships are too narrow for wheelchairs to go through.

When handicapped people try to go on cruises, they often encounter the steamship mentality, which is conservative and tradition-bound to an astonishing degree. Don't take it personally. It isn't that they don't want the handicapped—what they don't want is anyone or anything that might hamper the safe, uneventful operation of a ship. However, ship travel is a wonderful experience, and it pays to shop around for a line that is cooperative and can accommodate your needs.

Cruising is an area of travel where almost everyone uses a travel agent. For a handicapped person, it's even more important to do so because there are so many details that need to be checked. Consult the agent as early in the planning stage as possible and always provide complete information about your needs and limitations. That will give the agent time to find an appropriate ship that goes to the destinations you want to visit. Ships change home ports and itineraries from season to season, so you may have to make compromises if a ship you like doesn't follow your preferred itinerary.

The best ship for handicapped people is without question

# ACCESSIBILITY OF SOME MAJOR CRUISE SHIPS

| | Specially outfitted cabins | Wheelchairs fit at dining tables | Width of cabin doors; bathroom doors |
|---|---|---|---|
| **American Cruise Lines** | | | |
| M/V America | No | Yes | Cabin 21½″ (23″ with door removed); bathroom 19½″ (21¼″ with door removed) |
| M/V New Orleans | No | Yes | Cabin 22½″; bathroom 22½″ |
| M/V Savannah | No | Yes | Cabin 24″; bathroom 23″ |
| **American Hawaii Cruises** | | | |
| S.S. Constitution | No | Yes | Cabin 37½″; bathroom 20″ |
| S.S. Independence | No | Yes | Cabin 37½″; bathroom 20″ |
| S.S. Liberté | No | Yes | N/A; ship being renovated |
| **Commodore Cruise Line** | | | |
| Bohème | No | Yes | Both 25″ |
| **Cunard Line** | | | |
| Queen Elizabeth II | Yes | Yes | Standard 22″; some 25″ and 31″ |
| **Cunard/NAC** | | | |
| Sagafjord | No | Yes | Can admit wheelchairs |
| Vistafjord | No | Yes | Same |
| **Delta Line Cruises** | | | |
| Santa Maria | No | Yes | Cabin 24½″; bathroom 22½″ |
| Santa Magdalena | No | Yes | Same |
| Santa Mercedes | No | Yes | Same |
| **Delta Queen Steamboat Co.** | | | |
| Delta Queen | No | Yes | Cabin 24″; bathroom 21″, 2″ riser at entrance |
| Mississippi Queen | No | Yes | Same |
| **Eastern Cruise Lines** | | | |
| S.S. Emerald Seas | No | Yes | Cabin 27″; bathroom 23″ with 4″ sill |
| **Holland America Cruises** | | | |
| Rotterdam | No | Yes | All cabin and public rest room doors and public entrances wide enough for wheelchairs; cabin bathroom doors are not. |

| Width of elevator doors | Inaccessible public facilities | Medical certificate |
| --- | --- | --- |
| N/A* | None | No |
| N/A | None | No |
| N/A | None | No |
| Varies | None | Physician's release required if traveling alone |
| Varies | None | Same |
| Varies | None | Same |
| 28″ | Sports deck, theater | Depends on condition |
| At least 50″ | Sports deck, Q4 Room | Yes |
| Wide enough for wheelchairs | Night club, sports deck | Release necessary |
| Same | Same | Same |
| 36″ | None | N/A |
| 36″ | None | N/A |
| 36″ | None | N/A |
| 35″ | See "Comments" | Only in case of recent illness |
| 35″ | No elevator to sun deck and Jacuzzi pool; two steps to theater | Same |
| Over 36″ | Lavatories have 4″ sills | No |
| Wide enough for wheelchairs | None | No |

*N/A indicates that the information was not available.

| | Quota for wheelchairs | Companion required | Dog guides permitted |
|---|---|---|---|
| **American Cruise Lines** | | | |
| M/V America | No | Only if not self-sufficient | Yes, with advance notice |
| M/V New Orleans | No | Same | Same |
| M/V Savannah | No | Same | Same |
| **American Hawaii Cruises** | | | |
| S.S. Constitution | No | Only if not self-sufficient | No |
| S.S. Independence | No | Same | No |
| S.S. Liberté | No | Same | No |
| **Commodore Cruise Line** | | | |
| Bohème | 12 | Yes | No |
| **Cunard Line** | | | |
| Queen Elizabeth II | No | Only if blind | No |
| **Cunard/NAC** | | | |
| Sagafjord | No | Yes | Yes |
| Vistafjord | No | Yes | Yes |
| **Delta Line Cruises** | | | |
| Santa Maria | No | Yes | No |
| Santa Magdalena | No | Yes | Yes |
| Santa Mercedes | No | No | No |
| **Delta Queen Steamboat Co.** | | | |
| Delta Queen | No | Yes | No |
| Mississippi Queen | No | Yes | No |
| **Eastern Cruise Line** | | | |
| S.S. Emerald Seas | No | Yes | No |
| **Holland America Cruises** | | | |
| Rotterdam | No | No | No |

| Oxygen restrictions | Special menus | Comments |
|---|---|---|
| Portable tanks only | Yes, with two weeks' notice | Deckhands always available to assist |
| Same | Same | Same |
| Same | Same | Same |
| No | Yes. Return request form two weeks before sailing | Port of Kona not wheelchair-accessible |
| No | Same | Same |
| No | Same | Only Papeete and Tahiti wheelchair accessible |
| Yes | Low fat, low calorie, low cholesterol, no salt, diabetic; no kosher | |
| Not accepted if dependent on artificial lung | All diets catered to, minimum two weeks' notice | Arrangements can be made for renodialysis with passenger's own machine |
| Passengers must provide their own. | 30 days' notice | No wheelchair accessibility to tenders |
| Same | Same | Same |
| No | One day to two weeks' notice depending on diet | |
| No | Same | |
| No | Same | |
| Yes | 15 days' notice | *Delta Queen*'s age prohibits carriage of non-ambulatory individuals. Passengers with impaired sight or hearing welcome, but must share cabin with non-handicapped adult. |
| Yes | Same | |
| No passengers or visitors requiring oxygen or oxygen therapy allowed | Yes, with 30 days' notice | No wheelchair accessibility to tenders (applies to Little Stirrup Cay only) |
| Yes | Request when making reservations | |

| | Specially outfitted cabins | Wheelchairs fit at dining tables | Width of cabin doors; bathroom doors |
|---|---|---|---|
| **Home Lines Cruises** | | | |
| Atlantic | No | Yes | Cabin 25″; bathroom 19″; no turning space into bathroom |
| **Norwegian Caribbean Lines** | | | |
| Norway | Yes | Yes | Cabin 28½″; bathroom 23½″ |
| Skyward | No | Yes | Cabin 23″; bathroom 19¼″ |
| Southward | No | Yes | Same as Skyward |
| Starward | No | Yes | Same as Skyward |
| Sunward II | No | Yes | Cabin, bathroom 19¼″ |
| **Pearl Cruises** | | | |
| Pearl of Scandinavia | No | N/A | Cabin 21″; bathroom 24″ with 7″–9½″ sill |
| **Princess Cruises** | | | |
| Island Princess | 24 suitable, none specially outfitted | Yes | Cabin 22″ to 33″; bathroom narrower with 6″ sill |
| Pacific Princess | Same | Yes | Same |
| Royal Princess | 10; accessible bathrooms must be shared | Yes | Cabin 25″ to 31″; bathroom 22″ to 24″ |
| Sun Princess | Not advised for wheelchairs | Yes | N/A |
| **Royal Caribbean Cruise Line** | | | |
| Nordic Prince | No | Yes | N/A; step to bathroom |
| Song of America | No | Yes | Same |
| Song of Norway | No | Yes | Same |
| Sun Viking | No | Yes | Same |
| **Royal Cruise Line** | | | |
| Golden Odyssey | No | Yes | Cabin and bathroom 29″, step to bathroom |
| Royal Odyssey | No | Yes | Same |
| **Sun Line** | | | |
| Stella Oceanis | No | Yes | N/A; step to bathroom |
| Stella Solaris | No | Yes | Same |
| **Western Cruise Lines** | | | |
| S.S. Azure Seas | No | Yes | Cabin 21″; bathroom 21″ |

| Width of elevator doors | Inaccessible public facilities | Medical certificate |
| --- | --- | --- |
| 30″ | None | No |
| | | |
| Wide enough for wheelchairs | Very few | Depends on condition |
| Same | Same | Same |
| Same | Same | Same |
| Same | Same | Same |
| Same | Same | Same |
| | | |
| 30″ | Some | No, but inform line of disability at time of booking |
| | | |
| Wide enough for two wheelchairs | Observation Deck | Yes |
| | | |
| Same | Same | Yes |
| 35″ | Self-service laundry | Yes |
| | | |
| N/A | | Yes |
| | | |
| Wide enough for wheelchairs | Viking Crown Lounge | No |
| Same | None | No |
| Same | Viking Crown Lounge | No |
| Same | Viking Crown Lounge | No |
| | | |
| 30″ | Card Room, Bellevue Bar, Theater | No |
| Same as above | Sports deck, Theater | No |
| | | |
| Wide enough for wheelchairs | Sports deck, Lido Bar | Yes |
| Same | Same | Yes |
| | | |
| 33″ | Card Room, Casino, Video Arcade | No |

| | Quota for wheelchairs | Companion required | Dog guides permitted |
|---|---|---|---|
| **Home Lines Cruises** | | | |
| *Atlantic* | No | No | No |
| **Norwegian Caribbean Lines** | | | |
| *Norway* | No | Yes | Yes |
| *Skyward* | No | Yes | Yes |
| *Southward* | No | Yes | Yes |
| *Starward* | No | Yes | Yes |
| *Sunward II* | No | Yes | Yes |
| **Pearl Cruises** | | | |
| *Pearl of Scandinavia* | No | Yes | N/A |
| **Princess Cruises** | | | |
| *Island Princess* | Four | Yes | No |
| *Pacific Princess* | Four | Yes | No |
| *Royal Princess* | 10 | Yes | No |
| *Sun Princess* | Not advised for wheelchairs | Yes | No |
| **Royal Caribbean Cruise Line** | | | |
| *Nordic Prince* | No | Advised | No |
| *Song of America* | No | Advised | No |
| *Song of Norway* | No | Advised | No |
| *Sun Viking* | No | Advised | No |
| **Royal Cruise Line** | | | |
| *Golden Odyssey* | No | Advised | No |
| *Royal Odyssey* | No | Advised | No |
| **Sun Line** | | | |
| *Stella Oceanis* | No | Yes | No |
| *Stella Solaris* | No | Yes | No |
| **Western Cruise Lines** | | | |
| *S.S. Azure Seas* | No | Yes | Query line |

| Oxygen restrictions | Special menus | Comments |
|---|---|---|
| Prohibited | Two weeks' notice | |
| Maximum of eight E tanks permitted | Three weeks' notice | Passengers must bring collapsible wheelchairs. |
| Same | Same | Same |
| Same | Same | Same |
| Same | Same | Same |
| Same | Same | Same |
| N/A | One months' notice | Handicapped passengers are welcome, but rigorous shore excursions and configuration of ship cause difficulties for wheelchairs. |
| Approval by ship's physician | Two weeks' notice | Limited accessibility, but wheelchair passengers have been satisfied. |
| Same | Same | Same |
| Same | Same | All cabins can accommodate wheelchairs; private bathrooms not accessible. Several ports require tendering; not possible for wheelchairs. |
| Same | Same | |
| No, but inform line of technical details so staff can be helpful | No | Despite physical limitations, handicapped passengers have enjoyed cruises. |
| Same | No | Same |
| Same | No | Same |
| Same | No | Same |
| Yes | Three weeks' notice | Passengers must bring only 23″ collapsible wheelchairs with hard rubber tires. |
| Yes | Same | Same |
| Yes | All menus except kosher | |
| Yes | Same | |
| Must be cryogenic and approved by U.S. Coast Guard | No | Wheelchairs must be junior size (20″), folding |

Cunard's *Queen Elizabeth II*, popularly known as the *QE2*. Because it's so enormous, the passageways are wide enough for two wheelchairs to pass. It has built-in ramps and extra-wide doorways. Ten staterooms are specially designed for handicapped passengers. If more than ten such rooms are needed on a trip, the maintenance crew will adapt other rooms temporarily. The elevators are wide and the entire ship is accessible except for the top deck (sports deck) and the Q4 Room.

A group of twenty-six wheelchair passengers went on a cruise on the *QE2* from New York to Southampton, England. Because of its size the group encountered some architectural problems, but the crew was very helpful in building ramps where needed and in assisting people in difficult areas. The wheelchair group, by the way, participated in lifeboat drills along with all the other passengers.

Cunard requires a physician's letter from any handicapped person attesting to his or her fitness to travel. It isn't worth quibbling about—shipping lines often require such letters for the elderly and for pregnant women. Sometimes such a large ship as the *QE2* cannot enter a cruise port harbor and has to anchor in the roadstead outside the harbor. The passengers are taken to port on a tender, or small craft. Whether a handicapped person will be transported on a tender is an iffy question; in his letter the physician should mention whether he thinks this is possible or advisable. If the line tells you, when you make your reservations, that you are allowed to be taken on tenders, get it in writing, because the ship's officers may have different ideas. Dog guides are no longer allowed because of rabies regulations at some ports.

Costa Cruises, which operates the *Carla C.* and the *Daphne*, has had many handicapped passengers over the years who have completely enjoyed their cruise experiences. The line's policy is to assess the advisability of cruising for each prospective traveler on a case-by-case basis, taking into consideration the physical realities of the ships and the needs of the handicapped person. But the line lets prospective passengers make their own decisions about whether or not cruising is right for them.

Similarly, Paquet Cruises, operator of the *Mermoz*, makes special arrangements for handicapped passengers and treats each case individually. The ship has elevators and all rooms are fitted for heavy seas, meaning that there are railings and handles in strategic locations. Some areas are not accessible by wheelchair because of the vessel's size and design.

International Cruise Passengers' Association, an organization for people who love cruising, conducts regular cruise and ship inspections and provides special information for its disabled members. In addition to seeking out appropriate ships, it will research accessibility at ports of call. The club's report on 125 oceangoing cruise ships includes access ratings. The association publishes a bimonthly color tabloid, which occasionally carries a feature called "Gangway for the Wheelchair Crowd." A subscription is $12 per year. Write to ICPA/ Cruise Digest, P.O. Box 9, Bala Cynwyd, Pennsylvania 19004.

## TIPS FOR SHIP TRAVEL

Inside cabins, which have no portholes, are usually considerably larger than comparable outside cabins and are cheaper, too. If you don't suffer from claustrophobia, you can have room to turn around and save money in the bargain. In addition to the decks, ships have beautiful public rooms, so there's no reason to spend more time in your cabin than absolutely necessary. But if the thought of sleeping in a room without a window makes you queasy, you'd better class yourself as a claustrophobe and opt for an outside cabin.

If you are in a wheelchair, choose a cabin amidships, preferably near the banks of elevators. Not only will you have a smoother ride but, especially on leviathans like the *QE2*, you will eliminate miles and miles of pushing to get to and from the elevators. Ask to sit at a table near the entrance to the dining room—pushing on dining room carpet can be a chore. And remember to take advantage of the lavish outdoor luncheon and late-night buffets. Those plus midmorning and mid-afternoon snacks on deck make eating in the dining room optional.

Most importantly, if you are not pushing your wheelchair or being pushed, *put the brakes on!* An imperceptible roll of the ship can start your wheels going and you may be heading for the rail or into a bulkhead before you know it.

# 3

# AUTOMOBILES AND RECREATION VEHICLES

## AUTOMOBILES

A hand-controlled automobile is probably the single greatest aid to independence and mobility that a handicapped person can have. Transfer into the seat, pull the folding wheelchair into the back, and you're off without a worry—except, of course, for finding accessible accommodations, restaurants, and toilet facilities. You have to do some homework before starting on a trip to an unfamiliar area, and you have to be obsessive about checking information carefully. Just because you read it in a book—even this one—doesn't mean you can take anything for granted. Conditions change, establishments change hands, what is true this year may not be true next year. But the general trend is up, as business, government, and the public as a whole are becoming more aware of the needs of handicapped people.

Car rental is a new area that has been opened up to the handicapped. The businessperson and the vacationer now have the option of flying to a distant city and renting a hand-controlled car for local travel and sightseeing, thereby eliminating long, tiring trips and dependence on taxis or someone else to drive. When booking, be sure to specify whether you prefer right-hand or left-hand controls. Sometimes there is no option.

Avis has hand controls available in major cities in all parts of the United States, including Hawaii, and can provide them by special request at any of their locations. The customer should give two weeks' notice and preferably call during normal business hours, 9:00 A.M. to 5:00 P.M., for better service. Cars are standard-size two- and four-door models. There is no extra charge and free drop-offs are possible. The toll-free number for information and reservations is (800) 331-1212. Hand controls are also available in major Canadian cities. From the United States, call the international reservations number: (800) 331-2112.

Hertz has hand-controlled cars in twenty-two major cities, but only at airports in Boston, Dallas/Fort Worth, Miami, New York (JFK and LaGuardia), Los Angeles, Newark, and San Francisco. They are also available in New York at the company's 310 East 48 Street location. There is no extra charge for hand-control equipment, but it must be specifically requested at least five days in advance through Hertz's central reservations office. The toll-free number is (800) 654-3131. Hand controls are available for standard-size sedans but can usually be fitted to most other size cars. Drop-offs are possible only in three areas: between Baltimore and Washington, D.C.; between the suburbs of Boston and metropolitan Boston; and within the state of Florida. All other rentals equipped with hand controls must be returned to the original renting location. Customers who want to rent hand controls for cash are required to leave a $25 deposit (some cities may charge more) in addition to the usual cash deposit for the vehicle. They must also complete an application form. All such deposits are credited against the rental charges when the vehicle and hand controls are returned to the renting location. If you use any of the credit cards acceptable to Hertz, no cash deposit is necessary except in Florida, where a $45 deposit is always required.

National Car Rental can make hand controls available in thirty major cities in the continental United States on standard-size cars only. There is no extra charge. No drop-offs are allowed. It's best to make your reservation as early in advance as possible, but that will not necessarily guarantee the availability of a hand-controlled car at your destination. Specify right- or left-hand controls when making your reservation. National's toll-free number is (800) 227-7368 (it spells "car rent" on your telephone dial); in Minnesota (800) 862-6064. National has a VuPhone Telecommunications Device for the Deaf (TDD) to accommodate those with speech and hearing impairments. Callers using any other type of TDD or teletype machine can also connect with VuPhone. The toll-free number is (800) 328-6323 from anywhere in the continental United States (except Minnesota), Hawaii, Alaska, Puerto Rico, the Virgin Islands, or Bermuda. In Minnesota the number is (612) 830-2134. A specially trained reservations agent handles these calls.

In South Africa, car rental for the disabled is offered by Avis at its airport and downtown locations in Johannesburg, Cape Town, and Durban. Cars are BMW 518s adapted to provide brake and accelerator controls in one hand-operated lever. Reserve through any Avis office.

Other than in South Africa it is so difficult to rent a hand-controlled car outside the United States and Canada that we might just as well say it's impossible. However, you can get such a car abroad if you reserve with Auto-Europe in the United States or Canada. Get in touch with them at least six weeks in advance of your departure. Write Auto-Europe at Box 500, Yorktown Heights, New York 10598 or telephone: New York City (212) 671-6616; New York state (800) 942-1309; United States nationwide (800) 223-5555; Canada (800) 268-8810. If any of these lines is tied up, call collect (914) 962-5252.

If you're planning to tour Britain by car, write for a booklet called *Guide for the Disabled* to The Automobile Association, Fanum House, Basingstoke, Hants RG21 2EA, England. It includes information about accessibility of hotels and restaurants, parking, driving regulations, tolls, ferry service, and breakdown assistance. It covers England, Scotland, Wales, Northern Ireland, and the Irish Republic. Normally there's a small charge, but the association will probably send it to you free if you belong to a motor club that is affiliated with the Automobile Association (AA). If you have such a membership, you will receive courtesy roadside service from the AA, which includes breakdown service and touring assistance.

When reserving a specially equipped car, whether in the United States or abroad, *always* get written confirmation. If the reservations agent says, "Don't worry," that's a sure omen that something will go wrong. A written confirmation in your hand is a powerful persuader in case there's been a slip-up— and slip-ups tend to occur when your needs are anything but routine. Be sure to bring your own sign with the wheelchair symbol so that you won't have any problem using reserved parking areas.

The American Automobile Association (AAA) publishes an excellent ninety-four-page paperback book called *Handicapped Driver's Mobility Guide*, which contains recommendations on equipment and vehicle selection, referrals to manufacturers meeting standards established by the Veterans Administration, tips on equipment installation and maintenance, and a directory of companies and organizations in the United States and Canada with products or services for the handicapped driver. It is available at local AAA offices. They also can provide a list of overseas auto clubs that offer reciprocal services to AAA members. Write to AAA, 8111 Gatehouse Road, Falls Church, Virginia 22047.

For automobile travel in the United States, write to the President's Committee on Employment of the Handicapped, Washington, D.C. 20210 for a free booklet called *Highway Rest Areas for Handicapped Travelers*. It lists over eight hundred accessible rest areas in forty-eight states (Alaska and Hawaii don't have any). The areas contain all or most of these specifications: ramps instead of steps; wide doorways and easy-opening doors; wide aisles and corridors; toilet stalls that can accommodate wheelchairs and have doors that swing out; support bars in the stalls; lowered towel containers and mirrors; water fountains that are within reach of a person in a wheelchair; telephones mounted at the proper height in a barrier-free booth; paved, wide sidewalks and ramped curbs in the parking lot; and extra-wide parking places reserved for those in wheelchairs. Although the number of accessible rest areas has more than doubled since the previous edition of this booklet in the late 1970s, it is still remarkable how few accessible rest stops there are on the nation's major highways.

## RECREATION VEHICLES

The term *recreation vehicles* (RVs for short) covers a wide range of travel trailers, truck campers, and camping trailers, but the vehicles that most interest handicapped people are known as van conversions. This is how the Recreation Vehicle Industry Association (RVIA) describes them:

Van conversions are standard truck vans with interior space converted to living area. Most include collapsible or rigid roof extensions to provide more headroom. Although more compact than conventional motor homes, van conversions can contain all essential facilities and equipment for temporary living while traveling or camping. Prices vary with the number of options ordered.

You don't have to live in the van—you can use it for transportation the way Ironside used to do on television. It can be converted to allow a wheelchair to roll up a ramp or be raised on a lift at the side or the back. A passenger can remain in his wheelchair in the van and can even move around inside (when it's not moving). A van with living arrangements can open up a whole world of recreation because it lets a handicapped person participate in camping trips on an equal basis with able-bodied friends and family. Not many campgrounds have facilities for the handicapped, but with a van conversion, you bring your own. A number of handicapped people have become so enamored of this mobile way of life that they have traded up to the much larger vehicles called motor homes. These can be totally self-contained living units with full electrical, gas, and water systems, stoves, and refrigerators; handicapped-equipped sleeping, living, and storage space; television; air conditioning; dishwashers; microwave ovens; and more.

RVs on dealer lots throughout the country generally will not meet the needs of most handicapped people. However, many manufacturers now custom-build or modify RVs using such equipment as wheelchair lifts, accessible hand controls, special living facilities, and grab bars. RVs have been modified to accommodate even the most severely handicapped travelers.

The following is a sampling of firms that either build or

modify RVs for the handicapped or that manufacture and install equipment which makes it possible for handicapped people to use RVs. Those firms with an asterisk (*) are members of RVIA and all of their RVs carry an RVIA seal, which signifies the manufacturer has certified that the vehicle has been built to the American National Standard for Recreation Vehicles. The standard covers the electrical, heating, and plumbing systems of the RV as well as its fire and life safety features.

*Airstream, Inc.
419 West Pike Street
Jackson Center, Ohio 45334
(513) 596-6111
*Custom-built motor homes and travel trailers*

*Barth, Inc.
State Road 15 South
P.O. Box 768
Milford, Indiana 46542
(219) 658-9401
*Custom-built motor homes*

Beach-Craft Motor Homes Corporation
52684 Dexter Drive
Elkhart, Indiana 46514-9535
(219) 264-4178
*Custom-built motor homes*

Braun Corporation
1014 South Monticello
Winamac, Indiana 46996
(219) 946-6157
*Lifts for vans and motor homes*

California Custom Design (Red-E-Kamp Division)
Building 831A
Fabric Engineering Space Center
Mira Loma, California 91752
(714) 685-5215
*Paratransit units*

*Contemporary Coach
P.O. Box 152
Goshen, Indiana 46526
(219) 533-4161
*Customized vans and mini-motor homes*

*Coons Manufacturing, Inc.
2300 West Fourth Street
P.O. Box 489
Oswego, Kansas 67356
(316) 795-2191
*Custom-built motor homes*

Deluxe Homes
2800 West Farmington Road
Peoria, Illinois 61604
(309) 674-6131
*Mass-produced vans and motor homes*

*El Dorado RV, Inc.
1200 West Tenth, P.O. Box 266
Minneapolis, Kansas 67467
(913) 392-2171
*Paratransit buses, motor homes, wheelchair lifts*

*Esquire, Inc.
Rt. #1, Box 19925-M205
Edwardsburg, Michigan 49112
(616) 641-5194
*Mostly mini-motor homes*

*Foretravel of Texas, Inc.
811 NW Stallings Drive
Nacogdoches, Texas 75961
(713) 564-8367
*Class A motor homes; will also custom build*

*Gerco Corporation
P.O. Box 804
305 Steury Avenue
Goshen, Indiana 46526
(219) 534-3441
*Park Model handicapped unit*

Handi-Ramp, Inc.
P.O. Box 745
Mundelein, Illinois 60060
(312) 566-5861
*Manufactures ramps*

*Lifestyle, Inc.
307 South Pike
Bolivar, Missouri 65613
(417) 326-6234
*Van conversions*

Manufacturing and Products Services Corporation
7948 Ronson Road

San Diego, California 92111
(619) 292-1423
*Accessories for motor homes and vans*

*National Coach
130 West Victoria
Gardena, California 90248
(213) 538-3122
*Paratransit vans and motor homes*

Quality Coach
Route 309
Montgomeryville, Pennsylvania 18936
(215) 643-2211
*Custom-outfitted RVs*

Ricon Corporation
11684 Tuxford Street
Sun Valley, California 91352
(213) 768-5890
*Motor homes and vans, lifts, and hand controls*

R. J. Mobility Systems
715 South Fifth Avenue
Maywood, Illinois 60153
(312) 344-2705
*Equipped vans and motor homes*

Ted Hoyer & Company, Inc.
P.O. Box 2744
Oshkosh, Wisconsin 54903
(414) 231-7970
*Lifts*

Total Mobility
4060 Stewart Road
Eugene, Oregon 97402
(503) 686-9706
*Equipped vans and motor homes*

Transportation Design Technology
8049 Arjons Drive
San Diego, California 92126
(619) 566-8940
*Wheelchair lifts*

*Turtle Top, Inc.
P.O. Box 537
118 W. Lafayette Street
Goshen, Indiana 46526
(219) 533-4116
*Customized vans and mini-motor homes*

*Winnebago Industries, Inc.
Commercial Vehicle Department
P.O. Box 152
Forest City, Iowa 50436
(515) 582-3535
*Modified commercial vehicles*

For an expanded, continually updated list of firms that make and modify RVs for the handicapped, send a stamped, self-addressed long envelope to RVIA Publications Department, P.O. Box 2999, Reston, Virginia 22090. If you'd like to know more about RVs in general, send $1 plus $.75 postage and handling to Department AW at the above address and request "Living in Style . . . the RV Way," a twenty-page color introduction to the RV life-style. The booklet tells how to choose, finance, insure, and use RVs and contains a list of sources for camping and other RV-related information. For a free catalog listing all RVIA publications, send a stamped, self-addressed long envelope to RVIA's Department NR. If you want the list, the catalog, and "Living in Style," there is no need to send a self-addressed envelope.

The National Park Service now has jurisdiction over 333 recreation and wilderness areas in the United States. Their accessibility to handicapped visitors varies according to the physical characteristics of each area. Entry fees are waived for holders of the lifetime Golden Gate Access Passport, available free of charge to all qualified handicapped people. For information about the passport and other facilities for handicapped visitors, write to National Park Service, United States Department of the Interior, P.O. Box 37127, Washington, D.C. 20013-7127.

Over seven hundred commercially operated campgrounds around the United States and Canada are affiliated with Kampgrounds of America, which works to ensure that they maintain high standards of attractiveness, cleanliness, and safety. The organization also provides a great deal of information for campers or potential campers in its *Directory, Road Atlas and Camping Guide.* In addition to a complete list of member campgrounds in the United States and Canada (with maps), the publication includes over fifty pages of state highway maps. You can pick up a free copy at any KOA Kampground or order one through the mail by sending $2 to KOA, Inc., P.O. Box 30558, Billings, Montana 59114.

# 4

## ACCESS GUIDES, DESTINATIONS, AND VACATION IDEAS

Getting from here to there isn't necessarily the handicapped person's greatest problem in traveling. After all, public carriers are experts in transporting people—all people—from one place to another, and as we have seen, they are making greater efforts to accommodate all passengers, not just the able-bodied. Furthermore you may be able to use your own or a rented car. Frequently the question is not how to go but *where* to go, and what to do when you get there. Two things are necessary to make a destination agreeable: one, accessible facilities, and two, information about those facilities. Even in your own hometown, it is unlikely that you have gone around with a tape measure checking out entrances and rest rooms, counting steps, and figuring the angles of ramps. How much more irritating it is then in a strange place when part of your precious vacation or working time has to be spent finding out what is possible and what is impossible.

## ACCESS GUIDES

The closest thing to having your own private investigator is getting a good access guide to the places you're going to visit. More cities than you might think have them, but surprisingly few handicapped people are aware of how many access guides exist or where to get them.

One of the best sources of information is the *International Directory of Access Guides*, prepared by the staff of *Rehabilitation World*, the journal of the U.S. affiliate of Rehabilitation International, a global network of service to the disabled in sixty-two countries. Sources for access guides to places in twenty-one countries in addition to the United States and Canada are listed. The directory is available for $5.00 from Rehabilitation International USA, Access Guide Directory, Suite 704, 1123 Broadway, New York, New York 10010.

Many access guides are available to places in the British Isles, but there is not much in English on continental destinations. In addition, the standards of survey used to compile access guides vary widely. Some are based simply on mail questionnaires; others are based on personal inspections by disabled surveyors.

However, a breakthrough has been made as a result of a unique cooperative effort between two schools for boys in England—sixteen- to twenty-year-old disabled students from the Hephaistos School near Reading and able-bodied members of a Christian student group at St. Paul's in London. The boys at Hephaistos (named for the lame Greek god) are preparing for university education in spite of such disabilities as spina bifida, polio paraplegia, brittle bones, hemophilia, damaged heart valves, restricted growth, thalidomide conditions, cerebral palsy, muscular dystrophy, and conditions caused by accidents.

Over the past twelve years, teams of twenty to twenty-five of the students have joined together for expeditions to the Isle of Jersey, Norway, various parts of France, and Israel. Survey teams, each including at least one disabled member, have personally checked transport systems, railroad stations, ferries, hotels, hostels, chateaus, restaurants, museums, and other places that a traveler might visit during a holiday or business trip.

Guides currently available are *Access in London, Access in Paris, Access in Jersey, Access in the Loire* (in French and English), *Access at the Channel Ports,* and *Access in Israel. Access in London* is available for $4.95, plus $1.95 per order for postage and handling, from the British Travel Bookshop, 40 West 57 Street, New York, New York 10019; telephone (212) 765-0898. The others can be ordered from Gordon R. Couch, 39 Bradley Gardens, West Ealing, London W13 8HE, England. All but the London and Paris guides are free, but Mr. Couch, the volunteer editor, requests a donation of about five pounds to help with the costs of production and air-mail postage. Make checks payable in sterling to PHSP. The guides are also available from The Royal Association for Disability and Rehabilitation (RADAR), 25 Mortimer Street, London W1N 8AB, England.

RADAR is the best source for access guides to cities and towns in Great Britain. Costs range from twenty cents to $1 plus postage.

The list that follows covers the latest information available about access guides to the United States, Canada, Australia, Bermuda, the British Isles, Hong Kong, Israel, New Zealand, and Singapore. Hong Kong, Israel, and Singapore have somehow picked up the designation *English-speaking* in the world of tourism, probably because English is the second language of so many people in those countries. The access guides listed here are all free unless a charge is noted. It can't be stressed too often that even after you have your guide it's important to check on specific places by mail or telephone to be sure that information is up to date. A guide is, after all, just that—it points you in the right direction, but it can't do your traveling for you.

## UNITED STATES*

### Alabama

Birmingham, 35203: *Birmingham, Alabama—A Guide for the Aged and Handicapped;* The Mayor's Council for the Betterment of the Handicapped, 305 City Hall, 710 North 20th St.

Montgomery, 36198: *Access to Montgomery: A Guide for the Handicapped;* Alabama Governor's Committee on Employment of the Handicapped.

### Arizona

Phoenix, 85004; *Access, Valley of the Sun,* Guide to Phoenix, Scottsdale, Tempe, Mesa, Chandler, Glendale, Sun City and Vicinity; Easter Seal Society, 702 N. First St. Postage Fee: $1.

Tucson, 85711; *Access Tucson and Green Valley;* Easter Seal Society, 920 N. Swan Rd. Postage Fee: $1 (United States), $2 (other countries)

---

*Research failed to uncover access guides for some states.

## California

Berkeley, 94720; *Berkeley Access;* University of California, Physically Disabled Students' Program, 2515 Channing Way.

Eureka, 95501; *Access to Eurkea for the Handicapped;* Easter Seal Society, 3289 Edgewood, P.O. Box 996. Tel. (707) 445-8841

Inglewood, 90301; *Access Able L.A.* (Los Angeles and Greater Southern California); Daniel Freeman Center for Diagnostic and Rehabilitation Medicine, 333 N. Prairie Ave.

Los Angeles, 90036; *Around the Town with Ease;* Junior League of Los Angeles, Inc., Farmer's Market, Third and Fairfax. Postage Fee: $.54 in stamps only.

Los Angeles, 90009; *Guide to the Handicapped & Elderly—Los Angeles International Arpt;* City of Los Angeles Department of Airports, 1 World Way.

Oakland, 94612; *Let Your Fingers Do The Walking: An Access Guide to the Oakland/Berkeley Area;* Access California, Rm. 110 City Hall, 1421 Washington St. Fee: $6.00 plus tax and postage: $1.75 for single copy; $.50 each additional.

Palo Alto, 94303; *Getting Around in Palo Alto;* Social & Community Services Dept., 250 Hamilton Ave.

Sacramento, 95822; *The Source: The Resource Directory for the Physically Handicapped of Fresno County;* California Assn. for Physically Handicapped, P.O. Box 22552. Fee: $1.

San Diego, 92103; *A Step in Time;* Community Service

Center for the Disabled, 1295 University Ave. Tel. (714) 293-3500.

San Diego, 92101; *Freeways: The San Diego Directory for the Disabled Community;* Able-Disabled Advocacy, Inc., 861 Sixth Ave., Suite 610. Fee: $.50.

San Francisco, 94121; *Guide to San Francisco for the Disabled;* Easter Seal Society, 6221 Geary Blvd. Tel. (415) 752-4888.

San Jose, 95128; *Outdoor Access Guide to Santa Clara County* and *Wheeling Your Way Through San Jose;* Easter Seal Society, 1245 S. Winchester Blvd., Ste. 116. Tel. (408) 241-3331.

Santa Barbara, 93105; *Open Doors;* Easter Seal Society, 351 S. Hitchcock Way, Ste. B165. Tel. (805) 682-1112.

### Colorado
Denver, 80206; *Coalition Access Denver;* Sewall Rehabilitation Center, 1360 Vine St. Free if requested but donation of $4 appreciated to cover costs.

### Connecticut
Hartford, 06112; *An Access Guide for Greater Hartford;* Hartford Easter Seal Society Rehabilitation Center, Inc., 80 Coventry St. Tel. (203) 243-9741, or The Architecture for Everyone Committee, Greater Hartford Chamber of Commerce, 250 Constitution Plaza, 06103.

New Britain, 06051; *Your Key to New Britain;* New Britain Chamber of Commerce, Inc., 127 Main St. Self-addressed stamped envelope.

New Haven, 06510; *Access New Haven; Guide for the*

*Handicapped: Yale University;* New Haven Office of Handicapped Services, 270 Orange St.

New Haven, 06515; *Register of Architectural Survey Facilities;* Woodbridge Rotary Club, c/o Mite Corporation, 446 Blake St.

Stamford, 06902; *The Directory;* Easter Seal Rehabilitation Center for Southwestern Connecticut, 26 Palmer's Hill Rd. Fee: $1.

Waterbury, 06708; *Access Waterbury: 1977;* Easter Seal Rehabilitation Center of Greater Waterbury, 22 Tompkins St.

## Delaware

Media, Pennsylvania, 19063; *Guide to Delaware County (Del.) for the Handicapped;* Delaware County Easter Seal Rehabilitation Center, 468 N. Middleton Rd.

Georgetown, 19947; *Welcome Handicapped Visitors;* Delmarva Easter Seal Center, 204 E. North St. Tel. (302) 856-7364, or Rehoboth Beach Chamber of Commerce, Convention Hall, 19971. Tel. (302) 227-2233.

Wilmington, 19802; *A Guide to Northern Delaware for the Disabled;* Easter Seal Society, 2705 Baynard Blvd.

## District of Columbia

Washington, 20001; *Access Washington;* Information Center for Handicapped Individuals, Inc., 605 G St. NW, Ste. 202. Tel. (202) 347-4986. Fee: $1.

Washington, 20001; *The Deaf Person's Quick Guide to Washington (D.C.);* Alice Hagemeyer, c/o Martin Luther King Memorial Library, 901 G St. NW, Rm. 410.

Washington, 20036; *Memorandum: Easy DC Touring for Handicapped;* Washington Area Convention and Visitors Assn., 1129 20th St. N.W.

Washington, 20560; *Smithsonian: A Guide for Disabled Visitors;* Office of Public Affairs, Smithsonian Institution. In English and Braille and on cassette.

## Florida

Daytona Beach, 32014; *A Guidebook for the Physically Handicapped, Disabled Veterans, Senior Citizens and Visitors of the Greater Halifax Area;* The Palmetto Club Juniors, 1000 S. Beach St. Tel. (904) 252-8131.

Gainesville, 32602; *Access to Gainesville;* Gainesville Chamber of Commerce, 300 E. University.

Melbourne, 32901; *Accessibility Guide to South Brevard;* Easter Seal Rehabilitation Center, 450 E. Sheridan Rd. Tel. (305) 723-4474, or Melbourne Chamber of Commerce, 1005 E. Strawbridge Ave., 32901.

Miami, 33133; *Access Miami Guide;* City of Miami, Department of Recreation, Programs for the Handicapped, 2600 S. Bayshore Dr., P.O. Box 330708, Tel. (305) 579-3432.

Miami, 33130; *Miami. See It Like a Native;* Metro-Dade Dept. of Tourism, 234 W. Flagler St. Tel. (800) 327-9508 or (305) 579-4694.

Miami Beach, 33139; *Wheelchair Directory of Greater Miami;* Fla. Paraplegic Assoc., Inc., 1366 13th Terrace.

Orlando, 32830; *Orlando's Guide for the Handicapped;* Orlando Area Tourist Trade Assoc., Inc. P.O. Box 22051.

Orlando, 32814; *Greater Orlando Area Hotel/Motel/Resort Accessibility Guide;* Fleury Foundation, Box 19352. Ten-dollar donation plus thirty-nine cents postage requested.

Pinellas Park, 33565; *Accessibility Lower Pinellas County;* Easter Seal Rehabilitation Center, 7671 Hwy. 19.

Sarasota, 33580; *Guide for Physically Handicapped— Manatee & Sarasota Counties;* Happiness House Rehabilitation Center, Inc., 401 Braden Ave. Tel. (813) 355-7637.

Tallahassee, 32301; *Florida Sightseeing for Visitors with Limited Mobility; Getting Around Walt Disney World; Trout Pond Recreation for the Handicapped;* Contact: Florida Department of Commerce, 126 Van Buren St.

Tampa, 33610; *Guide to the Tampa Area;* Easter Seal Society, 2401 E. Henry Ave. (Send stamped reply envelope.)

## Georgia

Albany, 31701; *Guide to Albany;* Southwest Georgia Easter Seal Rehabilitation Center, 1906 Palmyra Rd. Tel. (912) 439-7061.

Atlanta, 30303; *Guide for Handicapped Visitors to Corps of Engineers Lakes in AL, FL, GA, NC, SC, VA;* Dept. of the Army, South Atlantic Division. Corps of Engineers, 510 Title Bldg., 30 Pryon St. SW.

Atlanta, 30318; *Guide to Augusta;* Easter Seal Society, 1900 Emery St. NW, Ste. 106.

## Hawaii

Honolulu, 96813; *Hawaii Travelers Guide; Kauai Travelers Guide; Maui Travelers Guide; Oahu Travelers Guide;*

Commission on the Handicapped, 335 Merchant St., Rm. 215. Tel. (808) 548-7606. Postage fee required for multiple copies.

Honolulu, 96815; *Hawaii Visitors Bureau Member Hotel Guide* (access indicated); Hawaii Visitors Bureau, Suite 801, 2270 Kalakaua Ave.

## Illinois

Carbondale, 62901; *Carbondale Guide for the Handicapped;* Easter Seal Society, 801 S. Oakland, P.O. Box 3429. Tel. (618) 457-3333.

Chicago, 60611; *Access Chicago;* Rehabilitation Institute of Chicago, Research Dissemination Dept., 345 E. Superior St. Fee: $3.

Chicago, 60666; *O'Hare Airport for the Handicapped & Elderly;* Department of Aviation, O'Hare International Airport, P.O. Box 66142.

Deerfield, 60015; *Access North Suburban Chicago;* League of Women Voters of the Deerfield Area, Box 124.

Springfield, 62706; *Handicapped Individuals Guide to Illinois Recreation Areas;* 405 E. Washington. Tel. (217) 782-6752.

Springfield, 62706; *Recreational Areas Guide;* Illinois Department of Conservation, 605 Wm. G. Stratton Building, 400 S. Spring St.

## Indiana

Evansville, 47715; *A Guide for the Handicapped—Evansville, Indiana;* Southwestern Indiana Easter Seal Society Inc., 3701 Bellemeade Ave.

Fort Wayne, 46807; *Access Fort Wayne;* The Allen County Society for Crippled Children and Adults, Inc., 2722 Fairfield Ave. Fee: $.50.

Indianapolis, 46204; *Access to Recreation: A Guide to Indiana State Parks and State Recreation Areas for the Handicapped Visitor;* Indiana Dept. of Natural Resources, Division of Public Information & Education, 615 State Office Building. Tel. (317) 232-4200.

Indianapolis, 46204; *Navigation Unlimited in Indianapolis;* Muscular Dystrophy Foundation, 615 N. Alabama St., Rm. 214. Tel. (317) 632-8255.

## Iowa
Dubuque, 52001; *A Guidebook of Accessible Places in Dubuque;* 1982 edition. Handicapped Persons, Inc., P.O. Box 361.

## Kansas
Topeka, 66603; *Facilities Directory—A Guide to Accessible Establishments;* Topeka Human Relations Commission, Division for the Disabled, City Hall, Room 54.

Topeka, 66609; *A Guide for the Disabled of Wichita;* Easter Seal Society, 3701 Plaza Dr. Fee: $.50.

## Kentucky
Murray, 42071; *Access Guide for Restaurant Facilities of Murray and Aurora, KY;* Murray State University, Dept. of Professional Studies—Rehabilitation Division. Tel. (502) 762-3821.

## Louisiana

Baton Rouge, 70806; *Baton Rouge: A Guide for the Handicapped;* Junior League of Baton Rouge, 4950-C Government St.

Metairie, 70011; *Access New Orleans: French Quarter Rolling Tour;* Easter Seal Society, 4631 W. Napoleon Ave., P.O. Box 8425. Tel. (504) 885-9960. Postage Fee: $.50.

## Maine

Augusta, 04333; *Maine Guide for Handicapped and Elderly Travelers;* Governor's Committee on Employment of the Handicapped, 32 Winthrop St. Tel. (207) 289-2141.

Portland, 04101; *Easy Wheelin', A Wheelchair Accessibility Guide to The City of Portland, Maine;* Leisure Center for the Handicapped, Y.M.C.A., 70 Forest Ave. Tel. (207) 773-5273. Fee: $1.50, free to disabled.

## Maryland

Baltimore, 21202; *Bright Lights, Harbor Breezes* (published by the Easter Seal Society of Central Maryland); Baltimore Office of Promotion & Tourism, 34 Market Place. Tel. (301) 752-8632.

## Massachusetts

Boston, 02201; *Access to Boston;* Mayor's Commission on the Physically Handicapped, Boston City Hall, City Hall Plaza.

Boston, 02114; *At Your Service;* Recreation Therapy Dept., Massachusetts Rehabilitation Hospital, 125 Nashua St. Fee: $1.

Fall River; *Greater Fall River Area Handbook for the Handicapped;* Fall River Chamber of Commerce, 101 Rock St.

West Springfield, 01089; *Access Guide to Hampden (County), Wheeling Through Springfield;* Easter Seal Society, 380 Union St.

Worcester, 01608; *Wheeling Through Worcester;* Easter Seal Society, 37 Harvard St.

## Michigan

Ann Arbor, 48104; *Access Ann Arbor;* Ann Arbor Center for Independent Living, 2568 Tackard. Fee: $5 plus $1.50 postage.

Flint, 48504; *Access: Greater Flint;* Easter Seal Society of Genesee and Shiawassee Counties, Inc., 1420 W. Third Ave. Tel. (313) 238-0475.

Lansing, 48912; *Access Lansing, Entree East Lansing;* Center of Handicapper Affairs, a Handicapper Advocacy Alliance, Inc. Agency, 1026 E. Michigan Ave. TTY and voice: (517) 485-5887. Postage Fee: $1.

## Minnesota

Rochester, 55901; *Access Rochester;* National Spinal Cord Injury Foundation, Box 136.

St. Paul, 55101; *Explore Minnesota Accessibility;* Minnesota Travel Information Center, Minnesota Office of Tourism, 240 Bremer Building, 419 North Robert Street. Toll-free tel. (800) 328-1461; in Minnesota, (800) 652-9747; in the Twin Cities area, 296-5029.

## Mississippi

Jackson, 39216; *A Key to Jackson for the Physically Limited*; Mississippi Easter Seal Society, P.O. Box 4958.

## Missouri

Columbia, 65211; *Access Bulletin for Columbia, MO*; University of Missouri-Columbia, Dept. of Family Economics and Management, 238 Stanley Hall. Tel. (314) 882-7836.

Kansas City, 64108; *Accessibility Directory: Kansas City*; Access, 3011 Baltimore.

St. Louis, 63108; *St. Louis Has It A to Z for the Handicapped*; St. Louis Society for Crippled Children, Inc., 4108 Lindell Blvd. Tel. (314) 652-7342.

## Montana

Great Falls, 59401; *Guide to Great Falls for the Handicapped*; Easter Seal Society, 4400 Central Ave., or Great Falls Area Chamber of Commerce.

Missoula, 59802; *Access Missoula*; Missoula Advocacy, 323 W. Alder St. Tel. (406) 549-5061.

## Nebraska

Omaha, 68154; *Accessible Buildings and Businesses in Omaha*; Easter Seal Society, 12177 Pacific St.

## Nevada

Carson City, 89710; *Access Carson City* and *Access Reno*; Governor's Committee on Employment of the Handicapped, State Capitol Complex.

Las Vegas, 89158; *Access Las Vegas*; Governor's Committee on Employment of the Handicapped, State Mail Room.

### New Hampshire
Portsmouth, 13801; *Access Portsmouth;* Division of Vocational Rehabilitation, 147 Congress St.

### New Jersey
Hackensack, 07601; *Guide to Hackensack for the Handicapped;* Associated Craftsmen, 171 Atlantic St. Tel. (201) 342-5739.

### New York
Albany, 12210; *Access to Capitaland, I Love New York;* Easter Seal Society, 194 Washington Ave. Tel. (518) 434-4103.

Albany, 12209; *New York State Thruway Facilities for Handicapped Traveller;* Chief Engineer, New York State Thruway Authority, 200 Southern Blvd.

Auburn, 13021; *Access Guide to Cayuga County;* Easter Seal Society, Genessee Mall, Genessee St. Tel. (315) 253-5387.

Binghamton, 13901; *Access Guide to the City of Ithaca;* Easter Seal Society, 33 W. State St. Tel. (607) 723-9572.

Brooklyn, 11201; *Catholic Churches and All Parochial Facilities in Brooklyn and Queens Accessible to the Handicapped;* Office of the Handicapped, Brooklyn Catholic Charities, 191 Joralemon St. Tel. (212) 596-5500.

Buffalo, 14205; *Tri-City Directory* (Buffalo, Lockport, Niagara Falls); Building Barriers Committee, Rehabilitation Assoc. of Western New York, P.O. Box 74.

Huntington, 11743; *Access Huntington;* Town of Huntington, Services for the Handicapped, Town Hall.

Latham, 12110; *I Love New York Travel Guides* (accessibility indicated); separate guides for upstate and New York City; Tourism, Box 992.

New York, 10023; *Accessibility Guide to Lincoln Center;* Lincoln Center Public Information Dept., 140 W. 65th St. Tel. (212) 877-1800.

New York, 10048; *Facilities and Services for the Disabled, Newark Int'l, La Guardia & Kennedy Int'l Arpts;* Port Authority of New York & New Jersey, Aviation Public Services Div., One World Trade Center, Rm. 65N. Tel. (212) 466-7503.

Rochester, 14604; *The People's Accessibility Guide to Greater Rochester;* Easter Seal Society, 55 St. Paul St. Tel. (716) 232-2540.

Syracuse, 13202; *Wheelin' and Dealin' in Syracuse;* Easter Seal Society, State Tower Building, 109 S. Warren St., Ste. 615. Tel. (315) 471-8005.

Utica, 13501; *Guide For the Physically Handicapped and Aged;* New York Easter Seal Society, 287 Genessee St. Tel. (315) 797-0980.

### North Carolina

Charlotte; Access Hotline (704) 373-0982—Building & Facilities Access Information for Charlotte.

Greensboro, 27402; *Guide for the Physically Handicapped;* Greensboro Chamber of Commerce, P.O. Box 3246. Tel. (919) 275-8675.

## Ohio

Akron, 44313; *Akron Area Guide for the Handicapped;* Easter Seals, 3105 W. Market St. Tel. (216) 836-9741.

Canton, 44707; *Guide to Canton for the Handicapped;* Goodwill Rehabilitation Center, 408 Ninth St. SW. Tel. (216) 454-9461

Cincinnati, 45216; *Greater Cincinnati Guidebook for the Handicapped;* Southwestern Ohio Easter Seal Society Center, P.O. Box 16070. Tel. (513) 821-9890.

Cleveland, 44103; *Access Guide to Cleveland;* Vocational Guidance and Rehabilitation Services, 2239 E. 55 St. Also from Easter Seal Society, 20475 Farnsleigh Rd., Shaker Heights 44122, and from National Council of Jewish Women, 3535 Lee Rd., Shaker Heights, 44120.

Sylvania, 43560; *A Guide to Toledo for the Handicapped;* Toledo Society for the Handicapped, 5605 Monroe St.

## Oregon

Portland, 97225; *Circling the City;* Junior League of Portland, 4838 SW Scholls Ferry Rd. Tel. (503) 297-6364.

Portland, 97219; *The Portland Guide for the Handicapped;* Robin Jacobs, P.O. Box 19471. Fee: $7.95.

## Pennsylvania

Erie, 16501; *Access Erie;* c/o Steady Strivers of Erie, Inc., 609 French St. ($1 donation appreciated).

Harrisburg, 17120; *Access Pennsylvania;* Pennsylvania Bureau of Travel Development, 416 Forum Building. Tel. (717) 787-5453.

Levittown, 19056; *Access Bucks County;* Bucks County Easter Seal Society, 2400 Trenton Rd. Tel. (215) 945-1730.

Philadelphia, 19107; *Guide to Philadelphia for the Handicapped;* Mayor's Office for the Handicapped, City Hall, Rm. 143. Tel. (215) 686-2798.

## Rhode Island
Providence, 02903; *Rhode Island's Handicapped Access Booklets;* Dept. of Community Affairs, Governor's Committee on Employment of the Handicapped, 150 Washington St. Tel. (401) 277-3731. TDD: (401) 277-3701.

## South Carolina
Columbia, 29201; *Access Columbia;* Greater Columbia Chamber of Commerce, 1308 Laurel St., P.O. Box 1360. Tel. (803) 779-5350.

## South Dakota
Pierre, 57501; *Wheelchair Vacationing in South Dakota;* South Dakota Tourism, 221 South Central. Tel. (800) 843-1930.

Sturgis, 57785; *Wheelchair Vacationing in the Black Hills and Badlands of South Dakota;* Black Hills, Badlands and Lakes Assoc., P.O. Box 910.

## Tennessee
Chattanooga, 37402; *Disabled Visitors Guide to the Chattanooga Area;* Chattanooga Area Convention & Visitors Bureau, 1001 Market St.

**Texas**

Austin, 78763; *Access Austin;* MIGHT, Chapter II, Box 5746.

Dallas, 75234; *"Access" Dallas Guide for the Handicapped* and *Guide to Dallas/Ft. Worth Airport;* Texas Easter Seal Society, 4300 Beltway Rd. Tel. (214) 526-3811.

Houston, 77030; *A Guide for the Handicapped;* Coalition for Barrier Free Living, 6910 Fannin, Ste. 120. Tel. (713) 795-4252.

Midland, 79702; *Getting Around Midland, A Guide to Midland for the Physically Handicapped;* Midland Chamber of Commerce, P.O. Box 1890. Tel. (915) 683-3381.

San Antonio, 78229; *Access San Antonio;* Bear County Easter Seal Society, 2203 Babcock Rd. Tel. (512) 699-3911.

**Utah**

Salt Lake City, 84111; *Access Salt Lake;* Division of Rehabilitation Services, Utah State Board for Vocational Education, 250 E. 500 South St.

**Virginia**

Norfolk, 23501; *Tidewater Access Guide for the Handicapped;* Norfolk Chamber of Commerce, 420 Bank St., Box 327.

Roanoke, 24012; *Accessibility Guide to the Roanoke Valley;* Easter Seal Society, P.O. Box 5496. Tel. (703) 362-1656, or City Clerk's Office, Municipal Building, 215 Church Ave., SW, Rm. 456, 24011. Tel. (703) 981-2542.

Williamsburg, 23187; *A Guide for the Handicapped;* The Colonial Williamsburg Foundation, Drawer C.

## Washington

Seattle, 98119; *Access Seattle;* Easter Seal Society, 521 Second Ave. W. Tel. (206) 284-5706.

Spokane, 99204; *Guide to Spokane Area for the Handicapped;* Easter Seal Society, 510 Second Ave. W. Tel. (509) 838-8353.

## Wisconsin

Madison, 53704; *The Access Guide for Persons with Physical Disabilities—Madison, Wisconsin;* Access to Independence, Inc., 1954 E. Michigan Ave. Tel. (608) 251-7575. Single copies—postage fee: $1.25; each additional copy— fee: $2.00 plus postage.

Milwaukee, 53210; *A Guidebook to Milwaukee for the Handicapped;* Easter Seal Society, 5225 W. Burleigh Ave. Tel. (414) 871-1270.

## CANADA

### Alberta

Calgary, AB, T2P 1M3; *Handibook Calgary* and *Handibook Edmonton;* Calgary Action Group of the Disabled, 815 First St. SW, Rm. 604.

Edmonton, AB, T5S 1K4; *Access Guide to Edmonton;* Canadian Paraplegic Association, Alberta Division, 18129-107 Ave. Tel. (403) 484-7725, Donation: $5 or more appreciated.

### British Columbia

Vancouver, BC, V6P 5Y7; *Guide to Vancouver;* Canadian Paraplegic Assoc., 780 SW Marine Dr. Fee: $1.50.

Victoria, BC, V8W 2Z2; *British Columbia Accommodation & Travel Information Guide* (accessibility indicated) and *Tourism British Columbia Travel Guide for the Disabled;* Ministry of Tourism; 1117 Wharf St.

## Manitoba

Winnipeg, MB, R3A 1M5; *Easy Winnipeg Wheeling;* Canadian Paraplegic Assoc., 825 Sherbrooke St. Fee: $1.

## Newfoundland

St. John's, NF, A1C 6C4; *Access: City of St. John's;* The Hub, Information Service, P.O. Box 4397. Tel. (709) 754-0352. Also, *Newfoundland Guide for the Handicapped.* Fee: $1.

## Nova Scotia

Halifax, NS, B3H 1R2; *Guide for the Handicapped;* Halifax, Dartmouth & Metropolitan Area, Canadian Paraplegic Assoc. Nova Scotia Division, Fenwick Place, 5599 Fenwick St. Tel. (902) 423-1277/7009.

Halifax, NS; *Halifax Restaurants and Beverage Rooms, A Guide for the Handicapped;* City of Halifax, Department of Social Planning.

## Ontario

Barrie, ON, L4M 4Z2; *Barrie Accessible Community Transportation Service;* District Association, 70 Collier St., Ste. 602. Tel. (705) 737-2304.

Burlington, ON, L7R 4B7; *An Accessibility Guidebook of Burlington;* Burlington Social Planning Council, 760 Brant St., Ste. 406A. Tel. (416) 639-4804.

Cambridge, ON, N1R 6H7; *Freewheeling Through Cambridge;* Cambridge Chamber of Commerce, 785 Coronation Blvd. Tel. (519) 621-8030.

Dryden, ON, P8N 2Y4; *A Guide for the Physically Disabled and the Elderly in the Dryden Area;* Dryden Handicapped Assoc., Inc., Rte. 1, Box 34.

Guelph, ON, N1H 3H9; *Accessibility Guide to Guelph;* Guelph Information, 161 Waterloo Ave. Tel. (519) 821-0632.

Hamilton, ON, L8H 6N6; *Access Hamilton;* Ontario March of Dimes, 495 Woodward Ave. Tel. (416) 547-9233. Fee: $1.

Kingston, ON, K7L 1A2; *A Guide to Kingston for the Disabled;* Social Planning Council of Kingston and District, 14 Princess St. Tel. (613) 542-7317.

Kitchener, ON, N2J 2A9; *Access Guide for Kitchener, Waterloo, Guelph, Owen Sound, Cambridge and Huron County;* March of Dimes, 141 Weber St. S. Tel. (519) 579-4280.

London, ON, N5Y 2V7; *London—A Complete City Guide;* Ontario March of Dimes, 627 Maitland St.

Niagara Falls, ON, L2E 4C9; *Niagara Falls—Accessibility Guide for the Physically Disabled;* Information Niagara, 5017 Victoria Ave. Tel. (416) 356-4636.

North Bay, ON, P1B 5A3; *A Guide for the Disabled;* North Bay Civic Hospital, Dept. of Rehabilitation Medicine, 750 Scollard St.

Orillia, ON, L3V 6H9; *Orillia's Dependent Minority;* Orillia and District Ability Association, P.O. Box 13. Tel. (705) 326-7855.

Oshawa, ON, L1J 2Y1; *Access Guide for the Disabled— Durham Region;* Ontario March of Dimes, Civic Auditorium, 141 Thornton Rd. S.

Ottawa, ON, K2C 3N2; *Accessibility Guide in the National Capital Regions* (Ottawa-Hull) and *Directory for the Physically Disabled* (Ottawa-Carleton); Rehabilitation Institute of Ottawa, 885 Meadowlands Dr., Rm. 403. Tel. (613) 224-1522.

Owen Sound, ON, N4K 5N3; *Access to Owen Sound;* Parents of the Handicapped, 3549 Bayshore Rd. E. Tel. (519) 376-0669.

Peterborough, ON, K9H 7B6; *Peterborough Guide for the Physically Handicapped;* Peterborough Disability Resource Center, c/o St. Joseph's Hospital, 384 Rogers St. Tel. (705) 743-4251.

St. Catharines, ON, L2R 2C7; *Accessibility Guide for the Physically Handicapped* and *Recreation Registry for Disabled Persons;* Ontario March of Dimes, 3 Lowell Ave. Tel. (416) 685-3781.

Sault Ste. Marie, ON, P6A 1M2; *Accessibility Sault Ste. Marie;* Ontario March of Dimes, 180 Gore St. Tel. (705) 949-1699. Fee: $.50.

Thunder Bay, ON, P7C 3V3; *Mini Guide for Handicapped Visitors to Thunder Bay;* Ontario March of Dimes, 135 Syndicate Ave. N.

Timmins, ON, P4N 7N6; *Accessibility Guide for Timmins, Schumacher, South Porcupine and Porcupine;* Chamber of Commerce, 916 Algonquin Blvd. E. Tel. (705) 264-4321.

Toronto, ON, M4G 3V9; *Accessible Places* (one guide for each Canadian province) and *Freewheeler of Ontario;* Canadian Paraplegic Assoc., 520 Sutherland Dr.

Toronto, ON, M7A 2E5; *Guide for the Disabled Traveller Ontario;* Ontario Travel, 900 Bay St., Queens Park. Tel. (416) 965-4008.

Toronto, ON, M5C 1E5; *Information for the Physically Handicapped;* Community Information Centre of Metro Toronto, 34 King St. E., 3rd Fl. Tel. (416) 863-0505.

Toronto, ON, M4H 1M5; *Toronto with Ease;* Ontario March of Dimes, 90 Thorncliffe Park Dr. Tel. (416) 425-0501.

Waterloo, ON, N2J 2A9; *Access Huron County, Access Kitchener/Waterloo, Access Owen Sound* and *An Accessibility Guide-Book of Kitchener/Waterloo;* Ontario March of Dimes, Ability Center, 141 Weber St.

Welland, ON, L3B 3W8; *Access for Welland and Pt. Colborne;* Ontario March of Dimes, 160 E. Main St. Tel. (416) 735-3463; 384-9885.

Windsor, ON, N9B 1C3; *Accessibility Guide to Windsor and Essex County;* March of Dimes, Unit C, 1695 University Ave. W. Tel. (519) 254-6314, and Help Services of Windsor/Essex County, Inc., 789 Wyandotte St. E. Tel. (519) 253-6351.

## Quebec

Montreal, H2Y 1B5; *Useful Information for the Handicapped* (in English and French); CIDEM-Tourism, 155 rue

Notre Dame est. Tel. (514) 872-3561. Also from The City of Montreal New York Office, 360 Lexington Ave., New York, New York 10017.

## Saskatchewan

Saskatoon, SK, S7K 2P7; *Guide to Saskatoon for the Handicapped; Prince Albert—Guide for Handicapped; Regina—Guide for Handicapped;* Canadian Paraplegic Association, Saskatchewan Division, 325-5 Fifth Ave. N. Tel. (306) 652-4644.

## AUSTRALIA

Balwyn, Vic. 3103; *Australian Accommodation Guide;* Disabled Motorists (Victoria), 7/42 Northcote Ave. Tel. 830-5108. Fee: $2. (Aust.).

Beechworth, Vic. 3747; *Northeast Victoria and Albury for the Handicapped;* Occupational Therapy Dept., Ovens and Murray Hospital for the Aged.

Canberra, A.C.T.; *Car Parking Spaces for the Disabled in Canberra;* Department of the Capital Territory, Traffic & Transport Branch, Wales Center.

Cowandilla, S.A. 5033; *Access Adelaide;* ACROD S.A. Committee on Access, Phoenix Society Inc., P.O. Box 112.

Curtin, A.C.T. 2605; *National Accommodation Guide for Disabled Travellers,* Dept. of Industry & Commerce, Canberra; *Sydney for the Handicapped; North-East Victoria and Albury for the Handicapped* and *Tasmanian Accommodation Guide for Disabled People;* Australian Council for Rehabilitation of Disabled, P.O. Box 60.

Epping, N.S.W. 2121; *Access Guide to Sydney;* ACROD N.S.W., P.O. Box 185. Price on application.

Geelong, Vic. 3220; *Geelong and the Barwon Region for the Disabled;* Council for the Disabled (Barwon Region). P.O. Box 850.

Hobart, Tas. 7001; *Holiday Tours for the Handicapped: A Guide to Day Tours for the Handicapped in Southern Tasmania;* Box 252C, G.P.O. Fee: $1.

Lenah Valley, Tas. 7008; *Hobart for the Handicapped;* Tasmanian Assoc. of Disabled Persons, Inc., 20 Creek Rd.

Melbourne, Vic.; *A Day in the Open;* Ministry of Conservation, 240 Victoria St.

Mosman, N.S.W. 2088; *Wheelchair Accessible Routes: Taronga Zoological Park;* Taronga Zoo, P.O. Box 20.

Nambour, Qld. 4560; *Access: Guide for the Disabled— Sunshine Coast Tourist Facilities;* Sunshine Coast Committee on Recreation for the Handicapped, Queensland Recreation Council, SGIO Building, Currie St.

Perth, W.A. 6000; *Guide to Perth for the Handicapped;* Council of Social Services of W.A. Inc., 76 Murray St.

Shenton Park, W.A. 6008; *Guide to Perth for the Handicapped;* W.A. Committee on Access and Mobility, c/o Independent Living Centre, Para Quad Association, Selby St.

South Oakleigh, Vic. 3167; *Gippsland for the Handicapped;* Gippsland Branch, and *Melbourne for the Disabled;* Victorian Association of Occupational Therapists, 24 Golf Rd.

Sydney, N.S.W. 2000; *Accommodation Directory;* Touring Dept. N.R.M.A., 151 Clarence St.; *Day Tours for the Disabled in and around Sydney;* 1981, N.S.W. Department of Tourism.

Warrnambool, Vic. 3280; *Warrnambool for the Handicapped;* Mr. R. Ziegler, Senior Occupational Therapist, Warrnambool Base Hospital.

Wembley, W.A. 6014; *A Guide to Perth's Picnic Sites, Parks and Ocean Beaches for Those with Restricted Mobility;* W.A. Department for Youth, Sport and Recreation, P.O. Box 66.

## BERMUDA

Hamilton 5; *The Access Guide to Bermuda for the Handicapped Traveller;* Richard Kitson, Society for the Advancement of Travel for the Handicapped, c/o Cranleigh Services Unlimited, P.O. Box HM 1822. Also from Bermuda Dept. of Tourism, 630 Fifth Ave., New York, NY 10111.

## CHANNEL ISLANDS (BRITISH)

London W13 8HE; *Access in Jersey;* Pauline Hephaistos Survey Projects, 39 Bradley Gardens. Donation to PHSP appreciated to cover costs of mailing and production.

## DENMARK

New York 10017; *Access to Denmark: A Tourist Guide for the Disabled;* Danish Tourist Board, 655 Third Avenue, and in major cities in other countries. Eighty-eight-page book on all aspects of tourism. Free.

## ENGLAND

London W1N 8AB; *Access to Cinemas and Theatres in Central London for Disabled People in Wheelchairs* and *Theatres and Cinemas: An Access Guide;* Access Guides to the Nature Reserves of England, Scotland and Wales; Access guides to numerous cities in the United Kingdom; Royal Association for Disability and Rehabilitation (RADAR), 25 Mortimer St. Tel. (01) 637-5400. Cost of postage requested (international postal money order for overseas inquiries).

London W13 8HE; *Access at the Channel Ports; Access in London;* Pauline Hephaistos Survey Projects, 39 Bradley Gardens. Donation to PHSP appreciated to cover costs of mailing and production (obligatory five-pound fee for *Access in London*).

New York 10019; *Access in London;* British Travel Bookshop, 40 West 57 Street, New York. Fee: $4.95 plus $1.95 postage.

## FRANCE

London W13 8HE, England; *Access in Brittany/the Loire/ Paris;* Pauline Hephaistos Survey Projects, 39 Bradley Gardens. Fee: Donation to PHSP appreciated to cover costs of mailing and production.

## HONG KONG

Hong Kong; *A Guide for Physically Handicapped Visitors to Hong Kong* and *Accessibility of Hotels in Hong Kong;* Rehabilitation Division Officer, Joint Council for the Physically and Mentally Disabled, Hong Kong Council of Social Services, G.P.O. Box 474. Also from Hong Kong Tourist Association offices in New York, Chicago, San Francisco and major cities in other countries.

## IRELAND

Dublin 4; *Guide to Dublin for the Disabled;* National Rehabilitation Board, 24-25 Cyde Rd.

Dublin 2; *Discover Ireland: Activities & Facilities for Disabled Persons* and *Ireland: Accommodation and Restaurant Guide for Disabled Persons;* Special Projects Dept., Bord Failte-Irish Tourist Board. Baggot Street Bridge. Fee: 30 p. each. Also available from Irish Tourist Board offices in New York, Chicago, San Francisco, Los Angeles, Toronto and major cities in other countries.

## ISRAEL

London W13 8HE; *Access in Israel;* Pauline Hephaistos Survey Projects, 39 Bradley Gardens. Fee: Donation to PHSP appreciated to cover costs of mailing and production.

## ITALY

Milton Keynes MK3 6HN, England; *Access in Rome;* Open University Students' Assoc., Sherwood House, Sherwood Drive, Bletchley.

## JAPAN

Tokyo 105; *Accessible Tokyo;* Japan Red Cross, Welfare Dept. 1-1-3 Shiba Daimon, Minato-ku.

## NETHERLANDS

New York 10017; *Holiday in Holland for the Handicapped;* Netherlands National Tourist Office, 355 Lexington Avenue, and in major cities in other countries.

## NEW ZEALAND

TE ARO, Wellington; *Accessible Accommodations in New Zealand;* New Zealand Crippled Children's Society, P.O. Box 6349. Tel. 845-674.

## SCOTLAND

Edinburgh EH4 3EU; *Accommodation with Facilities for Disabled Visitors;* Scottish Tourist Board, 23 Ravelston Terrace.

Edinburgh EH8 9HW; *Guide to Edinburgh and Lothian for the Disabled;* Edinburgh Committee for Coordination of Services for the Disabled, Simon Square Center, Howden St. Inquire about fee.

Edinburgh EH7 4QD; The major source of information in Scotland on all aspects of disability, including holidays, transport, sports, and recreation; Scottish Information Service for the Disabled, 18/19 Claremont Crescent. Tel. (031) 556-3882.

## SINGAPORE

Singapore 1024; *Access Singapore;* Singapore Tourist Promotion Board, Tudor Court, Tanglin Rd. Tel. 235-6611.

## WALES

Mid-Glamorgan CF8 1XL; *Disabled Visitors Guide to Wales;* Wales Council for the Disabled, Crescent Rd., Caerphilly. Inquire about fee.

## DESTINATIONS AND VACATION IDEAS

The destinations and vacation ideas discussed in the following pages were selected because they represent a cross section of interests common to travelers: major cities in the United States and abroad, historic areas and restorations, museums, theme parks, and outdoor activities. All of the places described are reasonably accessible to at least some handicapped people and all have taken steps in a positive direction to improve their facilities and provide information for handicapped visitors. All of these should be regarded as suggestions to be evaluated in the light of a handicapped person's particular needs and interests.

# UNITED STATES

CALIFORNIA
State law requires all buildings and facilities used by the public and constructed after 1970 to be accessible to the handicapped.

Anywhere in California, a curb painted blue signifies a designated parking space for the handicapped. These spaces are available to vehicles that display license plates identifying the driver as physically handicapped. Off-street parking spaces are marked with appropriate blue signs.

DISNEYLAND　　The following attractions plus all live entertainment areas can accommodate wheelchairs: Main Street Cinema, Mark Twain Steamboat, Shooting Arcade, Mission to Mars, America Sings, the Walt Disney Story featuring Great Moments with Mr. Lincoln, the Golden Horseshoe Revue, and World Premiere Circle-Vision. Several other attractions are accessible to the partially ambulatory. Most restaurants and shops have no steps or are ramped. The Plaza Inn has four steps. Special rest rooms are available in eleven locations. Write for *Handicapped Guest Guide* and other information to Disneyland, Guest Communications, 1313 Harbor Boulevard, Anaheim, California 92803.

LOS ANGELES　　Most hotels and tourist attractions have good accessibility. All facilities of the Los Angeles County Department of Parks and Recreation are completely accessible to the disabled. Reserved auto parking for the handicapped is found throughout the city. Public transit (SCRTD) has 1,370 wheelchair lift-equipped buses in service.

SAN FRANCISCO    The San Francisco Municipal Railway (MUNI) and Bay Area Rapid Transit (BART) are accessible to the disabled, including quadriplegics, but it helps to know your way around the system. Facilities include ramps, wheelchair entrance gates, elevators with Braille symbols, accessible rest rooms, telephones at low levels and with variable volume controls, and reserved parking for the handicapped at most stations. MUNI, the main city transportation system, comprises buses and trams as well as the famous cable cars. BART is the subway system to outlying areas. Write for handicapped guides to San Francisco Municipal Railway, 949 Presidio Avenue, San Francisco, California 94115; or telephone MUNI Accessible Service at (415) 558-2335. Call BART Passenger Service at (415) 465-4100, ext. 510 or 569.

The city has installed nearly three thousand ramps at crosswalks in every neighborhood shopping area as well as the downtown and civic-center areas. There is no way to push a wheelchair up and down the hills (some of them are almost impossible for walking), but the best means of seeing San Francisco is from the water anyway. The ferryboats to Sausalito and Tiburon are accessible and so are the sightseeing vessels used by Harbor Tours for around-the-city cruises. Information is available from Harbor Carriers, Pier 41 N/S, San Francisco, California 94133. Gray Line tour buses have storage space for wheelchairs, but advance notice is required. Write Gray Line, Inc., 420 Taylor Street, San Francisco, California 94102.

## COLORADO
Colorado means life in the outdoors—skiing, backpacking, horseback riding—and being handicapped is no handicap.

BRECKENRIDGE OUTDOOR EDUCATION CENTER (BOEC)    Just eighty-five miles from Denver on a thirty-eight-acre wilderness site, BOEC has year-round programs that include backpacking, camping, fishing, hiking, rafting, kayaking, rock climbing, orienteering, and natural history. Wintertime brings sit skiing, cross-country skiing, ice sledding, dog sledding, and winter camping. Courses of one day to three weeks are offered for students of all ages and physical capacities. Fees range from $30 to $75 per person per day and include equipment, food, lodging, and instruction. For information, write to BOEC, P.O. Box 697, Breckenridge, Colorado 80424.

WINTER PARK SKI AREA    The Winter Park Ski Area is renowned as the home of the Handicap National Championships in which participants compete in all skiing disciplines, including slalom, giant slalom, downhill, and cross-country. But all the champions started as beginners, many at Winter Park's Sports and Learning Center, which teaches over seven hundred people a week to ski despite more than thirty types of disabilities. Summer programs include hiking, camping, river rafting, sailing, nature study, and crafts. Winter Park's philosophy is best expressed by the director of its skiing program, Hal O'Leary, who says, "Handicapped people are often overprotected; they need to explore their outer limits, to feel the element of excitement." There is a five-dollar charge for lessons. For information write to Winter Park Sports and Learning Center, Inc., P.O. Box 36, Winter Park, Colorado 80482. Telephone (303) 726-5514.

## CONNECTICUT

MYSTIC SEAPORT      Located on the east bank of the Mystic River not far from New London, Mystic Seaport is a forty-acre outdoor maritime museum that seeks to preserve New England's maritime heritage and demonstrate its impact on the economic, social, and cultural development of America. Additionally, it is a charming semblance of a bustling nineteenth-century seaport and shipbuilding center—sort of a New England Williamsburg—put together from a collection of historic ships and buildings gathered from all over the Northeast. The staff of Mystic Seaport is acutely conscious of its drawbacks in accessibility and has formed a Handicapped Visitor Committee to grapple with the difficulties inherent in reconciling historical authenticity with accessibility for the handicapped. Unfortunately, the historically authentic fact is that handicapped people did not get around very much!

Right now, the nonhistoric buildings are being made accessible, but most historic buildings are not accessible. The ships cannot be boarded in a wheelchair. Admission for a person who is blind, in a wheelchair, on crutches, or deaf is $3 (regular admission for adults is $9). The reduced rate of $3 is also extended to the companion pushing a wheelchair. The following exhibits are accessible: North Boat Shed, Stillman Building, Figurehead Exhibit; Shaefer Gallery, Meeting House, Shipsmith Shop, Chandlery, Catboat Exhibit, Drug Store and Doctor's Office; Fishtown Chapel, School House, Oystering Exhibit, Mystic River Scale Model, Life-saving Station, *Australia* Exhibit, Lobstering Exhibit, and *Thames* Keel. All of these exhibits are coded with an H on the Visitor Map distributed at the entrances. The Galley, a fast-food restaurant, and the Seamen's Inne, for more elegant dining, are accessible. Rest rooms accessible to visitors in wheelchairs

are located on the grounds. The streets are authentically cob-
blestoned. All in all, you get at least your three dollars' worth.
For more information write Mystic Seaport Museum, Mystic,
Connecticut 06355. Telephone (203) 572-0711.

## DISTRICT OF COLUMBIA

SMITHSONIAN NATIONAL AIR AND SPACE MUSEUM    The Smithsonian National Air and Space Museum, opened on July 4,
1976, is the first museum built from the ground up to be
completely accessible. Wheelchair visitors can view the inside
of the Apollo 11 space capsule and the Spirit of St. Louis.
The visually impaired can hear descriptions of exhibits on
tape cassettes, and the deaf receive written scripts of the
movies and audiovisual displays. Elevators have Braille mark-
ings. Restaurants, rest rooms, and shops are fully accessible.
Oral and sign language interpreters are available, and there
are prearranged tours for the mentally retarded and the physically, visually, and hearing impaired. All tours must be arranged two to six weeks in advance. Write to National Air
and Space Museum, Scheduling Office, Office of Aerospace
Education and Publication, Washington, D.C. 20560. Telephone (202) 357-1400 (voice) or (202) 357-1729 (TDD).

An excellent booklet entitled *Smithsonian: A Guide for
Disabled Visitors* gives complete accessibility information about
the thirteen museums and the National Zoo that make up
the Smithsonian Institution. In addition to the Smithsonian
Institution Building, often known as the Castle, museums
covered are the Freer Gallery of Art, the National Museum
of American History, the National Museum of Natural History,
the National Museum of American Art, the National Portrait
Gallery, the National Air and Space Museum, the Hirshhorn
Museum and Sculpture Garden, the Arts and Industries Build-

ing, the Renwick Gallery, the Anacostia Neighborhood Museum, the National Museum of African Art, and the Cooper-Hewitt Museum (in New York City). Copies are free at all museum information desks or from the Office of Public Affairs, Smithsonian Institution, Washington, D.C. 20560.

TOURS OF THE CAPITAL     The White House provides guided group tours for the elderly and handicapped at 8:00 A.M. Tuesday through Saturday, except on Thanksgiving, Christmas and New Year's Day. Write for reservations one month in advance to Mrs. Carol McCain, Director of White House Visitors Office, 1600 Pennsylvania Avenue, N.W., Washington, D.C. 20500. Telephone (202) 456-2200. The best tours are congressional tours. You request these from your congressman. You don't have to know him—just contact his office in your home state. They are forty-five minutes long and depart from the East Gate on East Executive Avenue Tuesday through Saturday mornings at 8:15, 8:30, and 8:45.

UNITED STATES SENATE     Special tours offer signing for the hearing impaired and the opportunity for blind visitors to go beyond roped areas to touch displays and artifacts. Ramps and elevators ensure wheelchair access. Tours last about one hour and are adaptable to any group's age and intellectual level. Friends and relatives are welcome to accompany disabled individuals on these tours. It's best to make a reservation in advance. Write to Special Services, United States Senate, Office of the Sergeant at Arms, Room S-321, The Capitol Building, Washington, D.C. 20510. Telephone (202) 224-4048 (voice) or (202) 224-4049 (TDD).

Washington's rapid rail Metro system meets all federal laws governing accessibility. In addition to stations with elevators and trains with wide aisles to accommodate wheelchairs, the

Metrorail system offers substantial fare reductions and priority seating for the disabled. Some Metro buses are equipped with wheelchair lifts. For handicapped information call (202) 637-1245.

The Information Center for Handicapped Individuals maintains an up-to-date information bank on all aspects of handicapped access in Washington, including museums, hotels, restaurants, tours, sightseeing, and transportation. Write to them at 605 G Street, N.W., Suite 202, Washington, DC 20001. Telephone (202) 347-4986.

## FLORIDA

THE DARK CONTINENT, BUSCH GARDENS    In Tampa, The Dark Continent, Busch Gardens—a three-hundred-acre African-themed family entertainment center—is completely accessible except for The Brewery, a multistoried building with no access elevators. A single admission price includes all rides, shows, and attractions. Busch Travel Park, across from The Dark Continent, offers camping facilities for recreation vehicles. For information write The Dark Continent, Busch Gardens, P.O. Box 9158, Tampa, Florida 33674. Telephone (813) 971-8282.

WALT DISNEY WORLD    Walt Disney World (WDW) has paid special attention to the needs of handicapped visitors. In addition to special parking, vans with wheelchair lifts are available, usually on twenty minutes' notice. Day guests inquire at the Guest Relations window at the Transportation and Ticket Center; resort guests call Services in their hotels. Most restaurants and rest rooms are accessible and there are low-placed telephones. In the Magic Kingdom, all entertainment areas plus the following attractions can accommodate wheelchairs: Main Street Cinema, Tropical Serenade, Country Bear Jamboree, Diamond Horseshoe Revue, the Hall of Presidents, Liberty Square Riverboats, Mission to Mars, Circlevision 360, Magic Carpet 'round the World, Carousel of Progress, and Space Mountain. Locations of all handicapped facilities are shown in the free guidebooks available at the entrance. Of the WDW resort hotels outside the Magic Kingdom, The Polynesian Village is the most accessible, with forty-eight special ground-floor units in the Oahu building. For information write Walt Disney World, P.O. Box 40, Dept. GL, Lake Buena Vista, Florida 32830.

Guests who do not have their own cars and would like to see more of the Orlando area can use Handi-Cab of Florida, Inc., a special cab service for the handicapped. Write to them at 4210 West Cayuga Street, Tampa, Florida 33614. Telephone (813) 971-7411.

## HAWAII

Hawaii is a favorite destination of handicapped travelers, individuals and tour groups alike. Besides the islands' natural beauty and agreeable climate, the free-flowing, indoor-outdoor style of architecture that does away with many barriers has probably contributed to their popularity. Write for information (mention handicap) to Hawaii Visitors Bureau, 2270 Kalakaua Avenue, Honolulu 96815. Telephone (808) 923-1811.

Wheelchair taxi service—you don't need to leave your chair—is offered by Handicabs of the Pacific, P.O. Box 22428, Honolulu, Hawaii 96822. Telephone (808) 524-3866. The service is available for airport transfers, sightseeing, nightclubbing, shopping, or whatever else you like.

## MARYLAND

The revitalization of Baltimore, ignited by the development of Harborplace, the nation's first festival marketplace, extends to the provision of facilities and information for handicapped visitors. *Bright Lights, Harbor Breezes,* a free 104-page access guide, is the disabled visitor's key to accommodations, dining, attractions, sports events, theaters, and transportation. It is available through the Baltimore Office of Promotion & Tourism, 34 Market Place, Baltimore, Maryland 21202; tel. (301) 752-8632. Travelers will find the publication especially helpful when making reservations at one of the city's 153 wheelchair-accessible hotel rooms. For more personal assistance, contact the Handicapped Services Coordinator in the Mayor's Office of Human Development at City Hall by calling (301) 396-1915. In addition to providing accessibility information, this office can recommend sign interpreters for the deaf and readers for the blind, and make referrals to disability-related organizations throughout metropolitan Baltimore. Maryland Citizens for Housing for the Disabled can arrange "door-to-door" transportation, attendant care, and on-site logistical services for visitors. Call MCHD one month prior to visit at (301) 377-5900 or TTY (301) 377-4591. The city's Metro claims total wheelchair accessibility. Lift buses may be reserved in advance through the Mass Transit Administration at 109 East Redwood Street, Baltimore 21202. Telephone (301) 682-5438. Reservations must be made by 1:00 P.M. before the expected day of travel.

## MASSACHUSETTS

PLIMOTH PLANTATION    Plimoth Plantation, just north of Cape Cod and an hour's drive south of Boston, is an outdoor museum that re-creates Plymouth, Massachusetts, as it was in 1627. It is also the home of the Wampanoag Indian Summer Encampment. All outdoor exhibits, visitor centers, gift shop, and cafeteria are wheelchair accessible. The *Mayflower II* is not, but entrance is by a separate ticket. Twice a year, Plimoth Plantation offers sign language tours of the 1627 Pilgrim Village. For information write Plimoth Plantation, P.O. Box 1620, Plymouth, Massachusetts 02360. Telephone—voice or TTY—(617) 746-1622.

## NEVADA

LAS VEGAS    Las Vegas welcomes everybody and proves it by being remarkably well prepared to cater to handicapped visitors. Forget gambling for a minute; this entertainment capital in the middle of a desert offers luxurious hotel accommodations at remarkably low prices; terrific shows; good food of every description; a hot, dry climate tempered by universal air conditioning; side trips to such wonders as Hoover Dam and Lake Mead; and twenty-four-hour activity, in case you'd like to try sleeping all day and living it up all night.

A survey of Las Vegas's thirty top hotels has revealed that a handicapped visitor can expect to find several conveniences. By law public rest rooms must have stalls equipped for the handicapped, and there is usually a valet in attendance. There are ramps in many places, including entrances to casinos, restaurants, and show rooms and on some curbs. If there are no ramps and a person in a wheelchair is unaccompanied, all hotels have procedures for bellhops and security guards to provide assistance. It is, however, important to let the hotel know in advance so that personnel will be prepared. Advance notice is also important when making reservations for airline or bus tickets; tours (to Hoover Dam, for example); show rooms and lounges; restaurants and taxis. Since several conventions of handicapped people have been held in Las Vegas and an estimated 5 percent of the twelve million annual visitors are handicapped in some way, hotel staffs are knowledgeable and accommodating.

If a handicapped person is driving, it is best to make use of valet parking, since a parking space in a hotel parking lot may be a hundred yards from the entrance. All taxi companies have special procedures for helping the handicapped, so it's important to advise the cab dispatcher or bell captain when you order a cab.

The majority of Las Vegas hotels and motels have rooms equipped for the handicapped, but it's a good idea to check before making a reservation. Among the hotels so equipped (including for the blind) are: Caesar's Palace, Circus-Circus, Desert Inn, Dunes, Flamingo, Frontier, Hacienda, Las Vegas Hilton, Holiday Inns (three), MGM Grand, Mint, Riviera, Sahara, Sands, Showboat, Stardust, Tropicana, and Union Plaza, as well as some motels.

Blind visitors can expect to find that raised numbers are used on room doors and elevator buttons in almost all hotels and that dog guides are admitted everywhere. Some gambling tips: In blackjack, tell the dealer you are blind and he will flip and count your cards, then tell you what his "up" card is. You will have to tell a craps dealer what bets you want to make, but the number and play are always called out vocally in that game. In roulette, you will have to tell the dealer what you want to bet, and the number is always called vocally; the same in baccarat. In keno and bingo, it might be advisable to ask for some assistance or come accompanied, since numbers are called fast and keno tickets are hard to mark accurately. On some slot machines a jackpot will come up without any bells or buzzer. These big jackpots are paid by the hotel staff, not out of the machine.

For additional information, write Las Vegas Convention and Visitors Authority, P.O. Box 14006, Las Vegas, Nevada 89114.

## NEW YORK

NEW YORK CITY    Twenty major New York City museums offer gallery talks, walking tours, demonstrations, lectures, and film showings featuring sign language interpretation and subtitles. These are open to the general public as well as to the hearing impaired. For a schedule of events, send a stamped, self-addressed envelope to the Department of Education, The Museum of Modern Art, 11 West 53 Street, New York, New York 10019. For more information, call the TTY telephone number at the Museum of Modern Art, (212) 247-1230, or the TDD/TTY number at the Metropolitan Museum of Art, (212) 879-0421. The Museum of Modern Art, organizer of this program, is established in a building that is fully accessible, including the galleries, restaurants, bookstore, lavatories and auditoriums. For the visually impaired there are large-print brochures on major exhibitions and a "Please touch" sculpture garden.

The Metropolitan Opera offers several services to the blind, visually impaired, hearing impaired, and physically handicapped. Program notes for opera performances are available on audio cassette or in Braille on free loan. Each includes a synopsis of the opera, musical highlights, descriptions of the sets, costumes and staging, and notes on the composer and background of the opera. Cassettes, tape recorders, and Braille libretti may be borrowed from the Belmont Room before performances (ushers will provide direction and guidance). A limited number of score desk seats, previously available only to music students, can now be reserved through the Education Department by the blind and visually impaired. The seats are in an area with excellent acoustics but no view of the stage. Tickets are $5. Backstage tours include tactile exhibits and explanations of the creation of an opera production. Dog guides are welcome. Tour tickets are $5, $2 for students. Advance reservations are necessary. Call Backstage Tours, Metropolitan Opera Guild, (212) 582-3512.

An Infrared Listening System has been installed to provide greater clarity for audiences with hearing impairments (not total deafness). Lightweight cordless headphones that can be adapted to hearing aids or used alone are available on loan before performances for a fee of $1, with a major credit card or driver's license required for deposit.

For wheelchair patrons there are accessible lavatories on the dress circle level, ramps, and lowered water fountains. If you wish to stay in your wheelchair, mention this when making your reservation—some aisle seats can be removed. For reservations write Metropolitan Opera, Lincoln Center, New York, New York 10023, or call (212) 799-3100. For information about services for the handicapped call (212) 582-7500, ext. 462.

The New York City Opera, in its own beautiful house at Lincoln Center, offers these services: talking synopses, call (212) 925-1011; Braille libretti, call (800) 424-8567; detailed synopses for the hearing impaired, call (718) 763-6154 (TTY). An Infrared Listening System is also available.

Seats with prime sight and sound as well as a variety of preattendance services are offered by the Theatre Access Project of the Theatre Development Fund to encourage handicapped people to attend Broadway and off-Broadway performances. Free membership includes show offerings in regular and large print sent by mail, sign-interpreted performances once a month for selected shows, and some discounts on ticket prices. For an application form write to Lisa Carling, Theatre Access Project, Theatre Development Fund, 1501 Broadway, New York, New York 10036. Telephone (212) 221-0885.

In a city with few bargains the Shubert Organization offers wheelchair-bound theatergoers a fantastic deal. For $7.50 per ticket a disabled person and an accompanying adult will be admitted to any of the following Broadway theaters: Ambassador, Barrymore, Belasco, Booth, Broadhurst, Broadway, Cort, Golden, Imperial, Longacre, Lyceum, Majestic, Plymouth, Royale, Shubert, and Winter Garden.

## NORTH CAROLINA

FRENCH-SWISS SKI COLLEGE    Skiing has become the hottest sport in the South. The French-Swiss Ski College, the largest independent ski school in the United States, which annually hosts the Southeast Regional Special Olympics, has been very successful in teaching physically handicapped people to ski. For information write French-Swiss Ski College, Drawer 1250, Boone, North Carolina 28607.

## PENNSYLVANIA

SESAME PLACE    Sesame Place, a family play park strategically located within easy driving distance of Philadelphia and New York, is three and a half acres of sheer fun designed to stress ability, not limitation, in young and old, able-bodied and handicapped. Designed for youngsters from three to thirteen and their parents, it encompasses more than forty imaginative high-energy outdoor play elements plus an indoor "hands on" computer gallery and science center. Handicapped children (and adults) can play hide-and-seek in a forest of giant punching bags or roll out of their wheelchairs to bounce on a pillow of air or swim in a dry pool of featherlight plastic balls before going on to some satisfying learning experiences with computers and scientific equipment. Sesame Place is designed to stretch everyone's imagination with no barriers. Features include handicapped parking areas, accessible rest rooms, water fountains at three levels, free wheelchairs on loan, and ramps or elevators in every structure. For additional information write to Sesame Place, P.O. Box 579, Langhorne, Pa. 19047. Telephone (215) 757-1100.

## TENNESSEE

OPRYLAND     For country music fans, the Grand Ole Opry in Nashville is La Scala, the Met and Covent Garden all rolled into one glorious citadel of toe-tapping excitement. The Grand Ole Opry—the world's longest running radio show—is one part of the Opryland entertainment complex; other major aspects are the 120-acre Opryland U.S.A. theme park and the Four-Star Opryland Hotel. One admission fee covers more than a dozen live musical shows and all rides and exhibits. Admission to the Grand Ole Opry itself is covered by a separate ticket. There is a wheelchair location in the Opry House and rest rooms with wheelchair facilities are located in the Opry House and the park. With assistance from hosts and hostesses in the park, wheelchair visitors to Opryland U.S.A. can see every show and ride most of the twenty-one rides, including a white-water rafting adventure called the Grizzly River Rampage. The parking lot that serves both Opryland U.S.A. and the Grand Ole Opry has a special section for cars with handicapped passengers directly in front of the entrance gate. Wheelchairs are available for a nominal rental fee and can be reserved by calling Guest Relations. The Opryland Hotel has rooms for handicapped guests. For additional information and a copy of the special guide for handicapped guests, write Opryland U.S.A., 2802 Opryland Drive, Nashville, Tennessee 37214. Telephone (615) 889-6611.

## VERMONT

SHELBURNE MUSEUM    Thirty-five buildings from all over New England assembled in a village-like setting contain an astonishing collection of American folk art, artifacts, and social history that, in the words of its founders, "show the craftsmanship and ingenuity of our forefathers." There seems to be room on this beautiful site, seven miles south of Burlington, for everything, including the 892-ton steamboat *Ticonderoga*. While no pets are allowed on the grounds, dog guides, both seeing and hearing, are permitted. There are accessible rest rooms. Handicapped people are welcome, but many of the buildings have one or two steps at the entrance and narrow corridors. Write for information and wheelchair accessibility guide to Shelburne Museum, Inc., Shelburne, Vermont 05482. Telephone (802) 985-3344.

## VIRGINIA

COLONIAL WILLIAMSBURG    Almost everyone has heard of this living restoration of Virginia's Colonial capital, but you may not have realized that facilities have been provided to welcome handicapped visitors despite some of the barriers imposed by the eighteenth century. In fact, as the special brochure for the handicapped states, "eighteenth-century design offers advantages in some cases—there are few modern curbs in the Historic Area, and automobiles are not permitted on the main streets in the Historic Area most times of the day." Colonial Williamsburg operates three modern hotels, each of which offers one or more accommodations that are convenient for the handicapped. The Motor House has one specially equipped room, and most of the other rooms are on the ground level with parking outside the front door. The Lodge and Inn both have first-floor rooms and arrangements can be made for a special handicap. The brochure, *A Guide for the Handicapped*, gives detailed information about the accessibility of the Information Center, Historic Area, restaurants and rest rooms. It's free from The Colonial Williamsburg Foundation, Drawer C, Williamsburg, Virginia 23187. Hotel reservations may be made by mail to Reservations Manager, Drawer B, at the same address or by calling toll-free (800) 446-8956; in Virginia call (800) 582-8976.

THE OLD COUNTRY    This Busch Gardens theme park featuring eight authentically detailed seventeenth-century European villages is three miles east of Williamsburg and can conveniently be combined with a visit to Colonial Williamsburg. Six of the rides are not accessible or are ill advised for the non-ambulatory, but most of the attractions are accessible. Park policy prohibits employees from lifting an unaccompanied guest from a wheelchair. There are handicapped rest room facilities throughout the park and all restaurants are accessible. Dog guides are permitted. For information write to The Old Country, Busch Gardens, P.O. Drawer F-C, Williamsburg, Virginia 23187.

# EUROPE

## FRANCE

NATIONAL AUTOMOBILE MUSEUM    There has probably never been a hand-controlled Bugatti, but for devotees of classic automobiles just looking at one of these beauties is a thrill. In the town of Mulhouse in northeastern France 208 of these superb driving machines, including the renowned Bugatti Royale, are enshrined in the National Automobile Museum, two huge halls illuminated by nine hundred lamps modeled after those adorning the Pont Alexandre III in Paris. The museum houses other classic autos bearing such famous names as Ferrari, Lotus, and Maserati.

Special access for the handicapped is a feature of the museum, which includes a restaurant. The address is 192 Avenue de Colmar, 68200 Mulhouse, and it's open daily from 11:00 A.M. to 6:00 P.M. except Tuesday, Christmas and New Year's Day. For additional information write the French Government Tourist Office, 610 Fifth Ave., New York, New York 10020. Telephone (212) 757-1125.

## GREAT BRITAIN

Despite all the propaganda about British reticence, the fact remains that the British are probably the most *communicative* people in the world. Ask someone for directions and, instead of strangled grunts and lengthy gobbledegook interspersed with "You can't miss it," you'll be given clear, explicit instructions in as few words as possible (and often be escorted at least part way to your destination). If an elevator is out of order, you may find a sign next to it announcing the fact, explaining what's wrong with it, discussing what's being done about it, and giving an address or phone number in case you want to go into the issue more thoroughly!

There is a voluminous amount of general information available for the visitor to Britain, mostly from the British Tourist Authority and mostly free. But the special information that the handicapped traveler needs comes from a number of different sources and sometimes there is a charge for it, or at least for postage, so you may have to write a letter of inquiry before ordering what you want. Often the information is negative, but that's just as valuable as the positive. It is best to know definitely, for instance, that "buses and the underground railway systems are not effective means of transport for passengers in wheelchairs, since steps or escalators have to be negotiated."

Holiday Care Service, a nonprofit organization, acts as a central information service on holiday opportunities for people with disabilities. They can provide detailed London hotel information and answer other questions about accessibility in Britain for overseas visitors. Write to them at: 2 Old Bank Chambers, Horley, Surrey RH6 9HW (please enclose International Reply Coupons). Telephone: Horley (0293) 774-535.

LONDON    In London, you will find that taxis have twenty-four-inch-wide doors, clear floor space and plenty of headroom. But they are very high off the ground and many people find that they cannot transfer from a wheelchair unless they are willing to crawl onto the floor of the taxi. In this case, it is better to use the "mini-cabs," which are normal English-size cars (that is, small). Although mini-cabs don't cruise for fares, they can be ordered by telephone. One advantage is that you can order a mini-cab in advance to pick you up after the theater.

The theater is probably London's greatest attraction for the visitor and possibly its greatest pain in the neck for the disabled. Most of the theaters were built long before anyone thought much about the handicapped and are thus replete with flights of steps and inaccessible lavatories. In addition, there are complicated fire laws that sometimes have the effect of barring wheelchair patrons from accessible areas. Freda Bruce Lockhart, a prominent film critic and broadcaster confined to a wheelchair for many years, revealed in her excellent book, *London for the Disabled*, which, unfortunately, has been allowed to go out of print, that the Greater London Council has divided disabled people into three categories and evaluated theater accommodations for them accordingly.

The official categories are:

A. partially disabled persons able to walk, with or without assistance, from a wheelchair to a seat in the auditorium (may be unaccompanied, at the discretion of the management)
B. completely disabled persons unable to vacate their wheelchairs
C. disabled persons unable to walk, but able to remove themselves from a wheelchair to a seat in the auditorium, necessitating the chair being taken into the auditorium

Furthermore, "Disabled persons in categories 'B' and 'C' must be accompanied by an able-bodied adult capable of assisting him or her from the premises."

Miss Lockhart somewhat softens the effect of this information by commenting that "laws in England are seldom as rigid as they seem." But it is most important to telephone the theater manager in advance and explain the precise extent of your disability in terms of the categories listed above. Theaters are restricted to allowing anywhere from one to ten wheelchairs at a performance, so a spur of the moment decision to attend may end in disappointment.

The main source of information on access to London's theaters, cinemas, and other arts and entertainment venues is Artsline at 5 Crowndale Road, London NW1 1TU. Telephone: (01) 388-2227. RADAR (The Royal Association for Disability and Rehabilitation), 25 Mortimer Street, London W1N 8AB, England, publishes *Access to Cinemas and Theatres in Central London for Disabled People in Wheelchairs* and *Theatres and Cinemas: An Access Guide*. Visitors to London can order tickets in advance to plays, concerts, opera and ballet as well as to sporting events and exhibitions from Keith Prowse & Co. (USA) Ltd. There is a fee for the service, but the total will come to less than the cost of tickets for the Broadway theater. Keith Prowse representatives can check for you on the accessibility of these theaters and other venues of events for which they sell tickets. Write to them at 234 West 44 Street, New York, New York 10036. Telephone collect (212) 398-1430. Tickets to theatrical and musical performances only can also be ordered for a similar fee from Edwards & Edwards at One Times Square, New York, New York 10036. Telephone (800) 223-6108; in New York (212) 944-0290. Both agencies deal with the public as well as with travel agents.

The Museum of London is not only one of the city's latest must-see attractions—the two-thousand-year story of the people living by the Thames, from the Romans to the Blitz—but it is also accessible. It's a two-level modern building with 41,000 square feet of galleries situated three blocks north of St. Paul's Cathedral in the Barbican, a remnant of Roman Britain that was bombed out in World War II but has since been brilliantly revitalized. There are ramps throughout the two levels so that wheelchairs can pass easily, special toilets and elevators for the handicapped, and wheelchairs at the entrance. Admission is free. Don't miss it!

Guides to accessibility of some of London's traditionally popular tourist attractions in its oldest section are *The Tower of London, All Hallows Church and Tower Place* and *St. Paul's and Paternoster*. Write for copies to the City of London Information Centre, St. Paul's Churchyard, London EC4M 8BX, England.

The British Tourist Authority, at 40 West 57 Street, New York, New York 10019, and in major cities in other countries, can supply excellent free information about every aspect of tourism in Britain, including a pamphlet called *Britain for the Disabled*. The British Travel Bookshop at the same New York address has a large selection of guidebooks and maps for sale, including the excellent *Access in London* for $4.95 plus $1.50 postage. Write for its list of publications.

Guidebooks largely researched by and written for disabled people, including Will Forrester, the only Registered Guide who uses a wheelchair, are available at £2.25 from: Robert Nicholson Publications Ltd, 17 Conway Street, London W1P 6JD.

CHANNEL ISLANDS    Britain's Channel Islands are closer to France than they are to England. Their scenic beauty, balmy climate, superb food, and friendly people have made the islands of Jersey and Guernsey, as well as the mini-islands nearby, favorite haunts of British holiday-makers. Mobs of them descend from June through August. But in April and May, September and October and even during the mild winter, the islands are uncrowded and lovely—and inexpensive. An hour's flight from London takes you to Jersey, a bit longer to Guernsey. If you're in a wheelchair, do not try to fly between Jersey and Guernsey on Aurigny Air, the most frequent carrier, because its small planes are not accessible and it is unlikely their luggage capacity could even manage a folded wheelchair. British Airways flies large planes and you should have no more problems than usual.

Guernsey rises from the sea like Gibraltar and the streets above the harbor of St. Peter Port wind up hills as steep as San Francisco's. But the bustling life of the town is on the flat with restaurants and hotels facing the harbor. *Access in Jersey* gives detailed information about the larger (and sunnier) of the two islands, including hotels, restaurants, transportation, sightseeing, and public facilities. Information about all the Channel Islands is available from the British Tourist Authority, 40 West 57 Street, New York, New York 10019. Telephone (212) 581-4700.

## NORWAY

BEITOSTØLEN HEALTH AND SPORTS CENTER     The Beitostølen Health and Sports Center, 137 miles north of Oslo, is an exceptionally well-equipped sports facility for handicapped people. Among its features are an indoor swimming pool, sauna, gym room, rifle range, library, science room, 400-meter track, basketball court, archery range, riding trails and stables, rowing and trout fishing in an artificial lake, and ice skating (in wheelchairs) in winter. The area is a sanctuary for many species of birds.

Beitostølen, run by Erling Stordahl, who is blind, is the site of the annual Race for Light, a skiing competition for the blind that attracts hundreds of participants. Write for information to the Beitostølen Health and Sports Center, 2953 Beitostølen, Norway.

KVÅLE'S RIDING CENTER    For the real outdoor life, there is Kvåle's Riding Center at Fannrem in Orkdal, twenty-eight miles southwest of Trondheim. It consists of an inn with an open-hearth lounge and five log cabins especially designed for the handicapped. Each cabin contains four beds, running hot and cold water, toilet, electric heating, and cooking facilities. There are several riding horses and interesting trips can be arranged into the surrounding forest and mountains. There is good trout fishing in the summer and marked trails are ideal for Nordic ski touring during the winter. The owner, Amund Kvåle, is an experienced riding instructor from the Beitostølen Center. Write for a folder to Kvåle's Riding Center, N-7320 Fannrem, Norway.

# 5

# HOTELS AND MOTELS

With its ancient and honorable tradition of service to the public, the hotel industry would seem more likely than other facets of the traveler's world to understand and cater to the needs of handicapped guests. What you often find is that the spirit of the service is indeed willing, but the logistics may be weak. As Bob Eichel comments, "Hotels are often willing, but they don't know what to do." Or, even if they know what to do, it may be impossible to do it because of the architectural limitations of their buildings.

In some cases, a query from *Access to the World* has acted as a consciousness-raiser. For example, the manager of the Park Lane, a deluxe traditional hotel in London, commented, "We do have occasional guests in wheelchairs, but I now blush to think of some of their problems and how far we are from being fitted to help." The management of Asiaworld Hyatt Regency, under construction in Taipei, Taiwan, recommended to its owners that facilities for the handicapped be added, as did the Hotel Continental Mexico in Mexico City.

Sophisticated handicapped travelers may prefer charm and

tradition to standardized modernity, but the shiny new places are the ones most likely to be accessible. Patty Hughes says that the Savoy, for example, one of London's deluxe hotels, is terrible for a person in a wheelchair. "The dining room is seven steps down, the American Bar is twelve or fifteen steps up and the elevators don't stop at these funny in-between floors. Next time we stayed at a cheaper, modern hotel and had no problems."

As a rule, though, the higher class (and more expensive) the hotel, the more likely it is to be relatively barrier-free. Large elevators, large guest rooms, and large bathrooms all contribute to the comfort of people in wheelchairs, and these things don't come cheap nowadays. Operators of tours for the handicapped unanimously stick to first-class and deluxe hotels for overseas travel and, usually, the newer the better. Good motels are, of course, excellent choices because they are typically all on one level. The large motel chains, many of which have expanded into hotels also, have been in the forefront of adapting their properties to barrier-free design. Federal tax deductions of up to $25,000 are allowed to hotel, motel and resort owners for the addition of handicapped facilities at their properties.

Bathrooms are the biggest problem in hotels. They often have narrow doors, a step or sill in the entrance, not enough room for a wheelchair to turn around even if it can get in, not enough space to roll under the sink, no way to take a shower without getting in and out of a bathtub, and no grab bars near the tub and toilet. Removing the bathroom door is often a great boon to accessibility. If the bathroom is too small for the wheelchair to get in and you are able to lift yourself out of your chair, have a small straight-back chair—or, even better, a secretary's swivel chair with wheels—put into the bathroom and transfer onto it. If the bedroom is hard to maneuver in, have some furniture rearranged or moved out. When two people in wheelchairs share a room, it's almost always necessary to remove some furniture.

Handicapped people are usually cooperative and have a sense of humor about some of the adjustments they have to make to cope with barriers when traveling, but two things make them all see red—and they happen in hotels. Those are having to ride freight elevators or service elevators and having to be wheeled through the kitchen in order to reach restaurants, banquet rooms, and meeting rooms. Both are considered an indignity rather than an inconvenience and it really rankles. Whether anything can be done about this situation in older hotels is questionable, but one thing is certain—as time goes on, organizational meeting planners are going to be more aware of the needs of their handicapped members and will be loath to schedule functions in rooms with such extreme inaccessibility.

The major hotel and motel chains have established accessibility criteria for the properties they own or manage. Most of them publish a free directory identifying the properties that meet accessibility standards. All the hotels and motels listed in this chapter were selected because they were identified by their owners as having special rooms for the handicapped or other features that make them relatively accessible.

## BEST WESTERN

A property is identified by a handicapped symbol if it meets at least five of these eleven standards:

- minimum 32″ wide doorways/hallways
- ramps

- 27″ or lower sinks or vanity tops
- Braille-coded telephones or raised block-letter elevator buttons, menus, and guest room printed materials
- special menus for diabetics or those on salt-free diets
- handrail bars in bathroom
- reserved parking marked "Handicapped Only"
- guest room switches in convenient bedside locations
- drinking fountain 30″ high
- telephone equipped for hard of hearing
- other facility aids designed specifically for handicapped individuals

At the latest count, 392 Best Western properties in the United States and Canada had facilities for the handicapped. The toll-free reservation number is (800) 528-1234; in Arizona it's (800) 352-1222, TTY/TDD (800) 528-2222. For a copy of the latest *Road Atlas and Travel Guide*, write to Best Western International, P.O. Box 10203, Phoenix, Arizona 85064.

## DAYS INNS

There are three or four handicapped rooms for every one hundred standard rooms. In general, rooms in this chain, known for its economy pricing, have many accessibility features, including special parking areas or valet parking, bathroom grab bars, Braille elevator buttons, wide bathroom and closet doors, and accessible function rooms, public rest rooms, and swimming pools. Handicapped facilities are indicated in their directory, available by writing Days Inns of America, Inc., 2751 Buford Highway, N.E., Atlanta, Georgia 30324. Telephone (800) 325-2525.

## HILTON HOTELS CORPORATION
## (UNITED STATES ONLY)

Ninety-eight Hilton hotels offer specially equipped rooms for guests in wheelchairs. Most notable among them are the Atlanta Hilton and Towers with 144 such rooms, the Washington Hilton with 40, and the Las Vegas Hilton and the Flamingo Hilton (also in Las Vegas) with 30 each. Many properties also have facilities for the blind and deaf.

## HILTON INTERNATIONAL

There are facilities for the handicapped in most of these deluxe hotels. Specially equipped guest rooms include such features as a grab rail around the bath, a nonslip tub, doors wide enough for wheelchairs, and higher sinks. Several hotels have ramps at main entrances and accessible stalls in public rest rooms.

## HOLIDAY INNS

At least one specially designed room for the handicapped has been installed in all new properties since 1965 and older inns are required to install such rooms when constructing additions. Doors are wide enough for wheelchairs and bathrooms are arranged for moving around comfortably, including an easy fit for the wheelchair at the lavatory. Other standard features include grab bars and wall rails in the bathroom; swing bars above the tub, toilet, and bed; a light switch at bedside; and a specially marked parking space with an entrance ramp. For a copy of the *Holiday Inn Worldwide Di-*

*rectory* write to Holiday Inns, Inc., 3796 Lamar Avenue, Memphis, Tennessee 38195.

## HOWARD JOHNSON'S

Special rooms for the handicapped have doorways (including bathroom doors) that are thirty-two inches wide. Most Howard Johnson's Motor Lodge beds are four inches longer than standard size. The chain's toll-free reservations number is (800) 654-2000. In Oklahoma call (800) 522-9041. In Canada call collect (405) 848-8611. For a copy of *Lodging and Restaurant Directory* write to Howard Johnson, One Monarch Drive, Quincy, Massachusetts 02269.

## HYATT HOTELS CORPORATION
## (UNITED STATES ONLY)

All hotels have special rooms or can convert standard rooms quickly. Many have ten or more; the Hyatt Regency Milwaukee has forty-nine and the Hyatt Anaheim (just opposite Disneyland) has forty-two. The Hyatt Regency Maui in Hawaii provides wheelchair access maps to its three buildings and eighteen-acre property. In Lexington, Kentucky, the Hyatt Regency hosted the National Wheelchair Basketball Final Four Tournament with complete accessibility. The Hyatt Regency in Greenville, South Carolina, Hyatt Rickeys in Palo Alto, California, and Hyatt Regency in Princeton, New Jersey, are especially accommodating, the Princeton hotel featuring handicapped rooms with lowered closet rails and storage shelves, and door peepholes at wheelchair level.

## HYATT INTERNATIONAL

Almost all hotels are new and highly accessible even if specially equipped rooms are not available. But the specially equipped rooms are exceptional. In addition to bathtubs, they have stall showers, which many handicapped people consider a valuable convenience, since it eliminates the need for getting in and out of a bathtub, a feat in itself. The chain's toll-free worldwide reservation number is (800) 228-9000.

## MARRIOTT HOTELS

Every hotel offers specially adapted rooms, smooth or ramped entrances, accessible public rest rooms, Braille elevator buttons, and reserved parking. Virtually all public space is accessible to wheelchairs. Marriott's toll-free reservation number is (800) 228-9290; in Nebraska (800) 642-8008; TTY number is (800) 228-2489.

## QUALITY INNS INTERNATIONAL

Although each is independently owned and operated, all eight hundred establishments flying this banner must conform to corporate policy and have at least one handicapped room per one hundred guest rooms. Most of them exceed this ratio. Handicapped rooms have their switches, thermostats, and locks installed no more than forty-two inches from the floor. Bathrooms include tilt mirrors, two-way tub bars, straddle grab bars on toilets, and sliding pocket bathroom doors. Handicapped parking with ramp is also required. Optional facilities include remote control panel by the beds and in-room whirlpool baths with grab bars. Write for free directory to Marketing Department, Quality Inns International, 10750 Columbia Pike, Silver Spring, Maryland 20901. There is a toll-free TDD reservations number: 800-228-3323; in Maryland, (301) 681-8040.

## RAMADA INNS

The chain's directory indicates properties with wheelchair guest facilities, which include extra-wide doors, ramp entrances, and special equipment in rooms. Ramada's toll-free reservations number is (800) 228-2828. Write for the directory to Ramada Inns, Inc., P.O. Box 590, Dept. DB, Phoenix, Arizona 85001.

## RODEWAY INNS

Fifty out of 140 Inns have barrier-free rooms, which are indicated by the handicapped symbol in the chain's directory. Write for it to Rodeway Inns International, 2525 Stemmons Freeway, Suite 800/Dept. R, Dallas, Texas 75207. The chain's toll-free reservation number is (800) 228-2000.

## SHERATON HOTELS, INNS, AND RESORTS

Sheraton, with more than five hundred hotels in sixty countries, is a pioneer in adapting hotels for barrier-free access. Rooms termed accessible incorporate state-of-the-art features and either meet or exceed all existing codes and standards. To obtain information on handicapped facilities in specific

Sheraton properties and to make reservations worldwide, call toll-free (800) 325-3535 in the United States (including Hawaii and Alaska). From eastern Canada, call (800) 268-9393; from western Canada (including Newfoundland), call (800) 268-9330. For callers with hearing impairments, Sheraton's TTY/TTD reservation service is available toll-free in the continental United States (excluding Alaska and Hawaii) twenty-four hours a day, seven days a week, at (800) 325-1717. Additionally, Sheraton's Worldwide Directory notes which hotels, inns, and resorts have handicapped facilities. A copy may be requested by writing to the Sheraton Brochure Department, 60 State Street, Boston, Massachusetts 02109.


## WESTIN HOTELS

The Westin Ilikai in Honolulu has been praised for its accessibility by handicapped groups that have stayed there. Other hotels with a number of special rooms and/or other helpful features are the Century Plaza and The Westin Bonaventure, both in Los Angeles; The Westin Hotel, Renaissance Center, Detroit; and The Westin Galleria in Houston. Write for the chain's directory and brochure of handicapped facilities to Westin Hotels, The Westin Building, Seattle, Washington 98121. Westin's toll-free reservation number is (800) 228-3000.


The following hotels, which are not affiliated with chains, may be especially interesting to know about because they are either fully contained resorts or they are in places that are popular with vacationers.

# UNITED STATES

## ARIZONA

*The Wigwam*
Litchfield Park, Arizona 85340
Telephone: (602) 935-3811
Resort hotel all on one level. No stairs. Dining rooms, public rooms and guest rooms accessible. Grab bars in all bathrooms. Low telephones. Parking adjacent to main building and guest rooms. Level, well-lighted walkways on sixty-five landscaped acres.

## COLORADO

*Tamarron Resort*
P.O. Box 3131
Durango, Colorado 81301
Telephone: (800) 525-5420
No stairs to lobby. Portable ramps available where necessary. Guest rooms and public rooms accessible. Handicapped toilets in public rest rooms. Elevator doors open thirty-two inches. Elevator buttons and public telephones set lower. Parking accessible. Motorized golf carts for use on the grounds. Bellstand assistance if needed. Tamarron is classified as a handicapped facility.

## HAWAII

*Hotel Hana-Maui*
Hana, Maui, Hawaii 96713
Telephone: (808) 536-7522
All accommodations at ground level. One step to lobby. Din-

ing rooms and public rooms accessible. "We have had a number of wheelchair visitors and have had no real problems in catering to them."

*Kona Village Resort*
P.O. Box 1299
Kailua-Kona, Hawaii 96740
Telephone: (808) 325-5555; toll-free (800) 367-5290
Lobby at ground level, seven steps to dining room. Parking accessible. Accommodations in individual thatched bungalows, eight units have no stairs. Public telephones set lower. "Over the years, many, many people confined to wheelchairs have been able to enjoy the natural surroundings at Kona Village."

## ILLINOIS

*Inn of Chicago*
162 East Ohio Street
Chicago, Illinois 60611
Telephone: (312) 787-3100
Totally accessible to handicapped guests. Eleven handicapped-equipped guest rooms, ramped access to street level entrances. The hotel donates overnight accommodations, dubbed Rebound Rooms, to needy families of physically disabled patients at the nearby Rehabilitation Institute.

## LOUISIANA

*The Pontchartrain Hotel*
New Orleans, Louisiana 70140
Telephone: (504) 524-0581
Despite some of the barriers to be found in a traditional hotel,

the owner reports that "through the years we have been priviledged to welcome many physically handicapped and blind people. I don't believe that there is any situation we might face in serving the handicapped that we couldn't overcome."

## NEW HAMPSHIRE

*Mountain View House*
Whitefield, New Hampshire 03598
Telephone: (603) 837-2511
Eight steps to the lobby. No stairs to dining room and public rooms. Grab bars in about one-quarter of the bathrooms. Elevator doors open thirty-two inches. Elevators attended at all times. Public telephones set lower. Bellmen park cars.

## NORTH CAROLINA

*Pinehurst Hotel and Country Club*
P.O. Box 4000
Pinehurst, North Carolina 28374
Telephone: (800) 334-9560; in North Carolina (800) 672-4644
A gracious, spacious old-fashioned southern resort hotel that has kept pace with the times. Rooms and bathrooms are enormous, all public rooms are accessible, as are the main entrance and swimming pool. Guests in wheelchairs have been welcome for many years.

## PENNSYLVANIA

*Pocono Manor Inn & Golf Club*
Pocono Manor, Pennsylvania 18349

Telephone: (717) 839-7111
No stairs to lobby. Dining rooms and public rooms accessible via elevator. Elevator doors open thirty-two inches. Elevator buttons set lower. All areas of the inn accessible by elevators and ramps.

## SOUTH CAROLINA

*Hilton Head Inn*
Sea Pines Plantation
Hilton Head Island, South Carolina 29948
Telephone: (803) 785-5111
Three steps to lobby, ramp on one side. Dining rooms and public rooms accessible. Elevator doors open thirty-two inches. Ground level suites with patios open onto swimming pool. Some poolside rooms have bathroom grab bars. Wheelchairs also accommodated in ground floor, one-bedroom villas in Sea Pines Plantation. The beach at Hilton Head is long, flat and hard, hard enough to push a wheelchair on, even for someone with limited arm function. However, at the Hilton Head Inn, there are a few steps to go down to get to the beach.

## WEST VIRGINIA

*The Greenbrier*
White Sulphur Springs, West Virginia 24986
Telephone: (304) 536-1110
Ramp to lobby. Portable ramps available whenever needed. No steps to three main dining rooms. One step to Golf Club dining room. Service elevator to Tavern Room and Old White Club cocktail lounge. Public rooms accessible. Most bathrooms are large enough for wheelchair entry, some have grab

bars. Elevator doors open thirty-two inches. Elevator buttons set lower. Public telephones set lower. Valet parking. Many gardens and terraces will accommodate wheelchairs. Theater and meeting rooms accommodate wheelchairs. All stairs have rails. "We don't have Braille menus, but we have considerate waiters and waitresses."

## BARBADOS

*Best Western Sandy Beach*
Worthing
Christ Church
Barbados
Telephone: 89033
Five ground floor suites can be modified to provide access for wheelchair users and those suffering from cardiovascular and orthopedic disorders. There is a step to enter these suites but portable ramps are available as are bathroom grab bars, bed raisers, a transfer board, a floor-based trapeze bar, and portable hand-showers. Bathroom entrances may be too narrow for some wheelchairs, but management can remove bathroom doors if necessary.

Most public facilities—including swimming pool and restaurant—are on the same level and connected by nonslip paths wide enough for wheelchairs.

Additional information and reservations are available from Best Western: (800) 334-7234 in the United States; (800) 268-8993 in Canada; (416) 485-2632 in Toronto.

# GREAT BRITAIN

## LONDON

*New Berners Hotel*
Berners Street
London W1A 3BE, England
Telephone (01) 636-1629
Considered the most accessible hotel in London by Norman Wilkes Tours, it has won several awards, including one from the London Tourist Board. All public areas are accessible and there are special rooms for the handicapped.

*The Dorchester*
Park Lane
London W1A 2HJ, England
Telephone: (01) 629-8888
Four steps to lobby. Restaurant, grill room lounge, bar, reception, and key desk on ground floor level, no steps. Grab bars in bathrooms. Corridors and entrances to guest rooms and bathrooms are wide. Bathrooms large enough for wheelchair to turn. Elevator buttons and public telephones set lower. "We often have guests with wheelchairs and they find our front steps, with the aid of the carriage attendants or porters, easy to overcome."

# ITALY

## VERONA

*Albergo Due Torri*
Piazza Sta. Anastasi, 4

37100 Verona, Italy
Telephone: 045-595044
No steps to lobby. Full accessibility to restaurant and public rooms. Large guest rooms. Elevator doors open thirty-two inches. Elevator buttons and public telephones set lower. "Our staff is helpful when there are difficulties."

## LAKE COMO

*Plinio Casa Svizzera Hotel*
Evergreen Travel Service (representative)
19505 L Forty-fourth Avenue West
Lynnwood, Washington 98036
Telephone: (206) 776-1184
Located on the west side of Lake Como, near Milan, with an unobstructed view of the lake and mountains. Its rooms are all accessible with grab bars and lowered facilities. Bathrooms are accessible and wheelchairs can roll into showers. Accommodates forty-six guests with good food and friendly service. Has specially outfitted bus available for tours.

## JAPAN

## KYOTO

*Miyako Hotel*
Kyoto, Japan
Telephone: (075) 771-7111
No steps to lobby. All guest rooms and public areas accessible. Elevators have wide doors. Elevator buttons set lower. Evergreen Travel Service handicapped tour group stayed at hotel and reports being very pleased with service and facilities.

## TOKYO

*Hotel Okura*
3 Aoi-Cho, Akasaka, Minato-Ku
Tokyo 107, Japan
Telephone: (03) 582-0111
Elevator to fifth-floor lobby entrance. All restaurants and public areas accessible by elevator. Elevator doors open more than thirty-two inches. Attended elevators. Grab bars in bathrooms of deluxe twin rooms only. "We have 1,500 employees to assist you and make your stay enjoyable."

No matter what guidebooks and directories promise in terms of accessibility, hotels should always be queried individually, because people's needs are different and hotels do change from one year to the next. It's hard to think of any that has *ever* slipped *backward* in its facilities, so the good news is that you may sometimes be pleasantly surprised. It is important in this as in every aspect of travel to know what questions to ask, whether you are making arrangements for yourself, a friend, or a client. Use the following questionnaire as a guideline, substituting items that apply to your own situation:

### HOTEL/MOTEL QUESTIONNAIRE

Is there a handicapped parking area?_____Valet parking?_____
Can lobby be entered without using steps?_____
If there are steps, how many?_____Is a portable ramp available?____
Accessibility of restaurants, lounges, bars, meeting rooms, and other public rooms. Number of steps, if any; whether portable ramps are available.____

_____

_____

Are public rest rooms accessible without steps?_____

If not, have visitors in wheelchairs been able to use them?_____

Are there handicapped stalls in public rest rooms?_____

Is swimming pool accessible without steps?_____

Do elevator doors open at least 32 inches?_____

Are elevator buttons set lower?_____

Are public telephones set lower?_____

Is there a voice system announcing elevator floors?_____

Are there Braille elevator buttons?_____

Are there special rooms for the handicapped?_____

Are bathroom doors at least 32 inches wide?_____

If closets are walk-in, are doors at least 32 inches wide?_____

Is there a step or sill at the room door or bathroom door?_____

Do bathrooms have grab bars at toilet, tub, and shower?_____

Are there stall showers?_____Width_____Depth_____

Are there hand-held showers ("telephone showers")?_____

Can wheelchairs fit under bathroom sinks?_____

Are there Braille menus?_____Other Braille guides?_____

Are there amplified telephones?_____

Is there a TTY or TDD reservations system?_____

Are dog guides permitted? (Usually hotels/motels are required to accommodate them, by state law, but always check.)_____

For travelers to Europe and for travel agents, the *Guide Michelin* is indispensable, especially since it now indicates the accessibility of hotels. Individual volumes are available for all European countries and they all note the accessibility of hotels. The *Guide Michelin* criteria are:

- no steps or a single low step
- either an elevator or rooms available on the ground floor
- elevator dimensions at least $1.30 \times .80$ meters
- private toilet

- minimum width of doors to room and bathroom .75 meters
- minimum turning-around space in room 1½ meters × 1½ meters

This is definitely *not* the state of the art in accessibility, but for continental Europe it is at least a step in the right direction.

Order through your local bookstore or from Librairie de France, 115 Fifth Avenue, New York, New York 10003. It is the *red* guide you want for hotels—the green ones are for sightseeing.

The *Mobil Travel Guides* note hotels that have facilities for the handicapped and specify exactly what they are—ramps, wider doors, special toilets, etc. These guides cover the United States by region. Mobil now questions all establishments surveyed for the updated guides about handicapped facilities.

If you would like to go to Switzerland or are an agent sending clients there, the *Swiss Hotel Guide for the Disabled* offers accessibility information meticulously divided into three categories: (1) hotels for users of wheelchairs; (2) hotels for those who are severely handicapped in walking; and (3) hotels for those who are slightly handicapped in walking. It is available free from the Swiss National Tourist Office, 608 Fifth Avenue, New York, New York 10020.

A little pamphlet called *Memo to the Hotel Staff* is useful for anyone who would like to know the right way to treat a blind person, especially one with a dog guide. It is available free from The Seeing Eye, Morristown, New Jersey 07960.

# 6

# TOUR OPERATORS, TRAVEL AGENTS, AND TRAVEL ORGANIZATIONS

For most people there are three ways to go about making arrangements for a trip: (1) do it yourself; (2) tell a travel agent what you what and let him or her do it for you; or (3) buy a tour operator's preplanned tour from a travel agent.

It isn't quite so simple for a handicapped person. Obviously, doing it yourself requires a great deal of research, telephoning and letter writing, especially for overseas travel. Many people who have traveled widely and are sophisticated in the ways of the travel industry enjoy this kind of preparation almost as much as the trip itself. Besides, they feel that since they know their own needs and tastes better than anyone else, they would rather be in control of the planning from beginning to end. This is fine as long as one is well-organized, persistent, and meticulous about details. But for the first-time traveler—especially the handicapped one—doing it yourself could be an invitation to disaster.

Letting a travel agent make the arrangements for you, however, does not mean that you can simply dump everything in his or her lap and say, "Take care of it." Unfortunately there are only a few agents with any inkling of the needs of the handicapped. Bob Eichel, who was a travel agent for many years until he was stricken with muscular dystrophy, states flatly: "The average travel agency can't tell you anything concrete. Steps, handrails, bathroom for wheelchairs—they don't know." With very few exceptions, the handicapped person has to educate the travel agent about his special requirements while the agent, to function successfully, has to educate himself about the facilities available for the handicapped client. Ultimately this works out beneficially for both parties. Better service means more business because handicapped clients tend to be steadfastly loyal to really knowledgeable agents.

There is normally no charge for an agent's services. Agents make their money from commissions paid by carriers, hotels and other suppliers of travel facilities. (No, you don't get a discount if you make your own reservations.) Some agents charge a fee if they have to do an unusual amount of work for a client and the commissions involved are not adequate to cover all the time spent. This is an important point to check when establishing a relationship with an agent. And if you plan to travel with any frequency, you should be establishing a relationship, not merely doing business. Good rapport demands that clients be honest with agents about the nature of their handicap and specific about their needs, and that agents be attentive and genuinely interested in serving clients in a practical way.

While agents take care of reservations and ticketing for individuals, it is rare nowadays for an agent to tailor a complete vacation itinerary for only one or two people. Those who want to have all the details of a trip planned in advance usually buy a tour package that has been organized by a tour operator and is sold through local travel agents. In industry terms, a tour operator is a wholesaler and a travel agent is a retailer. However, in some cases an agent may organize a tour because there is a need for it among his clientele, and he may wholesale it to other agents. Some tour operators may function as travel agents by dealing with individuals who don't have access to a travel agency in their communities. This exchange of roles is often found in the case of special tours for the handicapped, where service to the client may demand that the traditional dividing lines be blurred.

The list that follows contains a mixture of travel agents, tour operators, and one nonprofit organization, all of which offer tours either solely for the handicapped or together with able-bodied people. Some have been working in this area for a long time and have developed a great deal of expertise; others have only recently become involved in it and have run only one or two tours but are interested in developing more in the future.

## DIALYSIS IN WONDERLAND

Don't be put off by the name. This is a remarkable project that originated at the Division of Artificial Organs of the University of Utah, but now operates from its own travel agency. This is a highly successful vacation adventure program for people on dialysis. Portable equipment and medical personnel go along on tours to Hawaii, Yellowstone National Park, the Grand Canyon, and other spectacular areas of the American West. Dialysis patients go rafting on the Colorado River, snowmobiling, jeep riding, fishing from a houseboat, hiking, water skiing—whatever any adventurer would like to do.

Patients gain an enormous sense of freedom from their usually constricted routines as well as improved physical strength and greater self-confidence. Family and friends are welcome but patients can go alone if they like. The program is also open to others with health limitations or handicaps who prefer to travel with a group that includes a physician, nurses, and medical supplies. Prices are kept to a minimum. Write for further information to Dialysis in Wonderland, 454 East 300 South, Salt Lake City, Utah 84111. Telephone (800) 423-8834 (in Utah, [801] 355-6039).

## ENCINO TRAVEL SERVICE, INC.

A retail travel agency that has been operating tours for the deaf since 1972, the Encino Travel Service has a mailing list of deaf people all over the country and has had many repeat customers. Tours have included Europe, China, the Soviet Union, Egypt/Israel, air-sea cruises to the Mediterranean, and river cruises in California. Prices include an interpreter for the deaf who acts as tour conductor. Encino sponsors a Weekend Adventurers Club for short trips around the Los Angeles area. The creator of and sales agent for these tours is Ruth Skinner, who is deaf herself. The agency has a teletype for the deaf, known as TTY. The TTY number is (818) 788-4515. If you want to "speak" to Ruth Skinner, call Monday or Wednesday between 9:00 A.M. and noon, but everyone in the agency knows how to use the TTY. For further information write to Ruth Skinner's Interpret Tours, Encino Travel Service, Inc., 16660 Ventura Boulevard, Encino, California 91436. The regular telephone number is (818) 788-4118.

## EVERGREEN TRAVEL SERVICE

The firm's Wings on Wheels tours have been operating since 1960, with more than a dozen tours a year now regularly scheduled for the blind, deaf, and physically handicapped. Since the tours stress not only accessibility but also a leisurely pace, as much as a third of the group is often made up of elderly people with no specific handicaps. Wings on Wheels goes in for glamorous destinations, such as the South Pacific, a Romanian health spa, Hawaii, luxury cruises, and even China, which is much in demand even though it presents many accessibility problems. Wings on Wheels requires that all clients be able to push their own wheelchairs on level ground and that the chairs be no wider than twenty-five inches and collapsible. Able-bodied friends and relatives are welcome on all tours. Arrangements can be made for a personal aide if necessary. For further information contact Betty Hoffman, Evergreen Travel Service, Inc., 19505 L Forty-fourth Avenue West, Lynnwood, Washington 98036. Telephone (206) 776-1184.

## FLYING WHEELS TRAVEL

Owned by Judd Jacobson, who is a quadriplegic, and his wife, Barbara, Flying Wheels operates several group tours for the handicapped every year but can also make suitable arrangements for individual travel. Since they know which airlines are most cooperative and which hotels are most accessible, and are aware of the many special needs of the handicapped traveler, they can perform this kind of service in a way that few agents are competent to do. They say that many clients all over the United States and in foreign countries have made

Flying Wheels "their personal travel agent." Among their most popular programs are "Best of England" and "Rose and Thistle" (England and Scotland.). These special-interest tours are designed for people in wheelchairs, those with visual and hearing impairments, and those with partial handicaps, such as heart conditions or diabetes. Families and friends are welcome. Trips move at a leisurely pace and are first class all the way, including such amenities as luncheons with owners of stately homes and backstage visits after musical and theatrical performances. For further information write to Flying Wheels Travel, 143 West Bridge, Box 382, Owatonna, Minnesota 55060. Telephone (507) 451-5005 or toll-free in the United States (800) 533-0363.

## HARBOR NEPHROLOGY ASSOCIATES

Cruises are arranged for dialysis and kidney-transplant patients aboard ships of Holland America Cruises to Alaska, Bermuda, the Caribbean, and Mexico as well as aboard the *Mississippi Queen* on the Mississippi River. Dialysis treatments and medical personnel are supplied by Harbor Nephrology Associates. Up to twelve patients can be accommodated, with a nephrologist and three or four nurses to monitor five dialysis machines. The ships provide the requisite low-potassium, low-sodium diets. Reimbursement for dialysis treatment is available under private insurance plans. Contact Harbor Nephrology Associates, 1032 N.E. Tenth Avenue, Fort Lauderdale, Florida 33304. Telephone (305) 462-7048.

## MENTOR INTERNATIONAL

Based in Jerusalem, this tour operator has run tours for handicapped Europeans and Israelis for several years. They now have a New York office and offer fully escorted tours to Israel for North Americans. Accommodations in first-class hotels and kibbutz guest houses are guaranteed totally accessible to wheelchairs, as are restaurants and sight-seeing areas. Transportation is by specially adapted motor coach that permits travelers to stay in their wheelchairs. Travel agents should contact Mentor International, Inc., 1 East 57 Street, New York, New York 10022. Telephone (212) 753-8393.

## TAKE-A-GUIDE

Britain's leading firm for individually tailored tours has a renowned service for handicapped clients. For those who can afford it, the luxury of a private car or limousine with a young driver-guide who may be an Oxford graduate, university lecturer, or linguist is probably the most comfortable and satisfying way of seeing Britain and the Continent in depth. Several of the driver-guides are also SRNs (state registered nurses). The company has had experience in serving handicapped clients since 1960. Various types of vehicles are used, ranging from small car to limousine to mini-bus. Write Take-A-Guide, Ltd., 63 East 79 Street, New York, NY 10021. Telephone (800) 223-6450; in New York (212) 628-4823.

## TAUCK TOURS

Summer helicopter hiking in the Canadian Rockies is a glorious adventure that is possible for anyone except the wheelchair-bound. From a cozy base lodge, adventurers are helicoptered deep into the heart of the Bugaboos or the Cariboos to traverse glaciers, amble across Alpine meadows and climb rocky escarpments surrounded by waterfalls and panoramic views. There are no roads, no trails. But there are extraordinarily skilled, patient mountain guides who have helped amputees, the blind, stroke and heart patients, and the very elderly to thrill to an achievement they had never thought possible—to experience the awesome beauty of a virgin wilderness. Heli-hiking, as it is known, utilizes the same comfortable lodges and helicopters that serve daredevil skiers in the winter. Eight- and nine-day trips depart from Calgary and include visits to Banff and Lake Louise. For information contact Tauck Tours, P.O. Box 5027, Westport, Connecticut 06881. Telephone (203) 226-6911.

## TRAVEL HELPERS LTD.

This retail and wholesale travel agency handles travel arrangements for wheelchair sports groups, amputee sports groups, blind sports associations, children's hospitals, and the Canadian National Institute for the Blind. It also works with individuals. Contact Travel Helpers Ltd., 160 Duncan Mill Road, Don Mills, Ontario M3B 1Z5, Canada. Telephone (416) 443-0583.

## VALLEY OAKS TRAVEL

Joan Diamond brings more than five years of experience in arranging travel for the physically disabled to her new program at this agency. She specializes in small groups and independent itineraries. France, Ireland, and Israel are destinations currently available. Information from Joan Diamond, Valley Oaks Travel, 13323 Moorpark Street, Sherman Oaks, California 91423. Telephone (818) 990-4560.

## WHOLE PERSON TOURS

Robert Zywicki, a former newspaper editor who has been disabled for most of his young life, and his wife, Elizabeth, have earned an international reputation for providing outstanding travel opportunities by assuring as much accessibility as possible during their tours and by affording individual attention to the needs of each participant. Offerings include Rome, Paris, Vienna, Amsterdam, Brussels, England, Scotland, Ireland, Scandinavia, Israel, and Egypt. A deluxe accessible motor coach will soon be available for tours of the continental United States. The Zywickis publish *The Itinerary*, the world's only magazine for disabled travelers. Subscription price for six issues a year is $7 ($9 for Canadian delivery). Write to Whole Person Tours, Inc., 137 West 32 Street, Bayonne, New Jersey 07002. Telephone (201) 858-3400.

## SOURCES OF INFORMATION

Among all the coupons you can clip from the Sunday travel section of your favorite newspaper, it is seldom that you will find one that offers to send you up-to-date or even slightly warmed-over news about travel for the handicapped. But there are a few sources from some highly specialized information that, if all pieced together, may prove useful.

## ACCENT ON INFORMATION

Affiliated with the excellent magazine for the disabled, *Accent on Living*, this is a computerized information retrieval system that can turn up material on practically every subject of interest to handicapped people. There is a $12 charge for the information retrieval plus $.25 per photocopy page. Ask for the Travel and Touring Category when you write to Accent on Information, P.O. Box 700, Bloomington, Illinois 61702.

## CYNERGY

As a consultant on travel for special populations, the organization provides consulting and training services for the tourist industry, government, and educational institutions on travel for the handicapped. Its book *The Handicapped Traveller: A Guide for Travel Counsellors*, by Cinnie Noble, is a comprehensive resource book for travel agents who would like to improve their skills in serving clients with various disabilities. It is available for $5 (Canadian) from the Canadian Institute of Travel Counsellors, 2333 Dundas Street West, Toronto, Ont. M6R 3A6, Canada. Telephone (416) 534-6301. Most of the information is applicable outside Canada.

## MOBILITY INTERNATIONAL USA

This is a newly established American branch of an international organization dedicated to fostering travel, educational exchange, and leisure activities among disabled and able-bodied young people in twenty-two countries. Programs include an information referral service, international conferences and work camps, an educational exchange, and a pen-pal clearinghouse. Work camps mean serious work no matter what the disability, as well as plenty of fun and comradeship with young people from other countries. The organization publishes a quarterly newsletter as well as *A World of Options: A Guide to International Educational Exchange, Community Service, and Travel for Persons with Disabilities* and *A Manual for Integrating Persons with Disabilities into International Educational Exchange Programs*. An audio-visual presentation, "Challenge Yourself and Change the World," is available for rent or purchase. For information write MIUSA, P.O. Box 3551, Eugene, Oregon 97403. Telephone (503) 343-1284 (voice and TDD).

## THE OUTSIDERS CLUB
An organization of more than eight hundred members throughout the British Isles and abroad that enables handicapped, shy, and isolated people to reach out to one another by mail, telephone and, if desired, in person with emotional and loving involvement in mind. It is nonprofit and confidential, run by volunteers in the London office who handle correspondence and maintain a postal library. They also offer help with aspects of disability, sexuality, relationships, shyness, and personal effectiveness. New members receive a list of all the other members in the club—their names, addresses, ages, difficulties and assets, hopes and desires. Nonthreatening social events are organized. The club is registered in England by The Social Habilitation and Integration Trust for Disabled People. For more information write to The Outsiders Club, Box 4ZB, London W1A 4ZB, England. Telephone (01) 741-3332 (twenty-four-hour line).

## SOCIETY FOR THE ADVANCEMENT OF TRAVEL FOR THE HANDICAPPED (SATH)

SATH is an organization of travel agents and tour operators interested in learning how to serve the handicapped traveling public more competently. The society hopes to serve as an industry clearinghouse to disseminate information about services and facilities presently available and to encourage the elimination of barriers and the adoption of a positive approach in the travel industry toward the handicapped traveler. For more information send a self-addressed, stamped envelope to SATH, 26 Court Street, Brooklyn, New York 11242. Telephone (212) 858-5483.

## TRAVEL INFORMATION SERVICE

Established by one of the nation's foremost facilities for the treatment of the physically handicapped, the service, for a moderate fee, will supply information to help disabled people plan trips in the United States and abroad. Its extensive library includes accessibility information about hotels and motels, cruise ships, airlines, historical sites, tourist attractions, and cities and countries around the world. The service's resources and data are constantly growing as travelers report back on their trips so that others can benefit from their experiences. The Travel Information Service is part of Moss's Regional Resource and Information Center for Disabled Individuals, a consumer information service on all topics of interest to the handicapped. Write to Travel Information Service, Moss Rehabilitation Hospital, Twelfth Street and Tabor Road, Philadelphia, Pennsylvania 19141. Telephone (215) 329-5715.

For general tourism information, write to the appropriate government tourist offices listed below. It is a good idea to ask if they have any information for the handicapped—the more requests they get, the more likely they are to make such material available. The countries listed are those that tourists seem most interested in visiting.

## Australia
Australian Tourist Commission, 489 Fifth Avenue, New York, New York 10017

## Austria
Austrian National Tourist Office, 500 Fifth Avenue, New York, New York 10110

## Belgium
Belgian National Tourist Office, 745 Fifth Avenue, New York, New York, 10151

## Bermuda
Bermuda Department of Tourism, 630 Fifth Avenue, New York, New York, 10111

Bermuda Department of Tourism, 1075 Bay Street, Toronto, Ontario M5S 2B1, Canada

## Canada
Canadian Consulate General-Tourism, 1251 Avenue of the Americas, New York, New York 10020

## China (People's Republic of)
China National Tourist Office, 60 East 42 Street, New York, New York 10165

## Denmark
Danish Tourist Board, 655 Third Avenue, New York, New York 10017

## Finland

Finnish Tourist Board, 655 Third Avenue, New York, New York 10017

## France (also Saint Pierre and Miquelon islands, Reunion Island, French Guiana, French West Indies, New Caledonia, Tahiti)

French Government Tourist Office, 610 Fifth Avenue, New York, New York 10020

French Government Tourist Office, 1 Dundas Street West, Toronto, Ontario M5G 1V3, Canada

## Germany (Federal Republic of)

German National Tourist Office, 747 Third Avenue, New York, New York 10017

German National Tourist Office, 2 Fundy, Place Bonaventure, Montreal, Quebec H5A 1B8, Canada

## Great Britain

British Tourist Authority, 40 West 57 Street, New York, New York 10019

British Tourist Authority, 94 Cumberland Street, Toronto, Ontario M5R 3N3, Canada

## Greece

Greek National Tourist Organization, 645 Fifth Avenue, New York, New York 10022

## Hong Kong

Hong Kong Tourist Association, 548 Fifth Avenue, New York, New York 10036-5092

## India

Government of India Tourist Office, 30 Rockefeller Plaza, New York, New York 10112

Government of India Tourist Office, Royal Trust Tower, Toronto, Ontario M5J 1A4, Canada

## Ireland

Irish Tourist Board, 757 Third Avenue, New York, New York 10017

Irish Tourist Board, 69 Yonge Street, Toronto, Ontario M5E 1K3, Canada

## Israel

Israel Government Tourist Office, 350 Fifth Avenue, New York, New York 10001

Israel Government Tourist Office, 102 Bloor Street W., Toronto, Ontario M5S 1M8, Canada

## Italy

Italian Government Travel Office, 630 Fifth Avenue, New York, New York 10011

Italian Government Travel Office, 3 Place Ville Marie, Montreal, Quebec H3B 2E3, Canada

## Japan

Japan National Tourist Organization, 630 Fifth Avenue, New York, New York 10111

Japan National Tourist Organization, 165 University Avenue, Toronto, Ontario M5H 3B8, Canada

## Mexico

Mexican Government Tourism Office, 405 Park Avenue, New York, New York 10022

Mexican Government Tourism Office, 101 Richmond Street West, Toronto, Ontario M5H 2E1, Canada

## Monaco

Monaco Government Tourist Office, 845 Third Avenue, New York, New York 10017

## Netherlands

Netherlands National Tourist Office, 355 Lexington Avenue, New York, New York 10017

Netherlands National Tourist Office, 327 Bay Street, Toronto, Ontario M5H 2R2 Canada

## New Zealand

New Zealand Government Tourist Office, 10960 Wilshire Boulevard, Los Angeles, California 90024

New Zealand Government Tourist Office, 630 Fifth Avenue, New York, New York 10111

## Norway

Norwegian Tourist Board, 655 Third Avenue, New York, New York 10017

## Philippines

Philippines Ministry of Tourism, 556 Fifth Avenue, New York, New York 10036

## Portugal

Portuguese National Tourist Office, 548 Fifth Avenue, New York, New York 10036

Portuguese National Tourist Office, 1801 McGill College Avenue, Montreal, Quebec H3A 2N4, Canada

## Spain

Spanish National Tourist Office, 665 Fifth Avenue, New York, New York 10022

Spanish National Tourist Office, 60 Bloor Street West, Toronto, Ontario M4W 3B8, Canada

## Sweden

Scandinavian Tourist Board, 655 Third Avenue, New York, New York, 10017

## Switzerland

Swiss National Tourist Office, 608 Fifth Avenue, New York, New York 10020

Swiss National Tourist Office, P.O. Box 215, Commerce Court Station, Toronto, Ontario M5L 1E8, Canada

## Thailand

Tourism Authority of Thailand, 5 World Trade Center, New York, New York 10048

## Union of Soviet Socialist Republics

Intourist, 630 Fifth Avenue, New York, New York 10111

## West Indies
Caribbean Tourism Association, 20 East 46 Street, New York, New York 10036

## Yugoslavia
Yugoslav National Tourist Office, 630 Fifth Avenue, New York, New York 10111

# 7

## YOUR GOOD HEALTH

Advice about staying healthy while traveling is usually based on the assumption that the travel in question is to foreign parts with potentially dire consequences from unfamiliar food, water, and bacteria. It is true that within the United States and Canada there are nearly universal standards for pure food and water, and there are few diseases that are peculiar to only one or two regions, but the wise traveler realizes that the mere fact of being away from his home environment may make him susceptible to minor upsets and infections from perfectly harmless sources. For example, San Francisco's undoubtedly hygienic drinking water may produce such symptoms as upset stomach and skin rash in a visiting New Yorker—and the other way around. A vacationer overtired from a long trip may develop a cold he never would have gotten had he stayed home. Consequently, even the strictly domestic traveler can profit from some of the advice to follow, which does, indeed, deal mainly with foreign travel.

In order of priority for a trip abroad, after reservations and a passport, a visit to a physician is a good idea—not to stock up on prescriptions for every ailment known to man or to be immunized against every conceivable bacterium or virus but because so many medical precautions and palliatives are highly individual. Almost every generalization has to be followed by the caution "Check with your own physician." Any specific medication suggested in this chapter is only an example of a *type*. For instance, don't take aspirin if it makes you sick, but do get an appropriate substitute. See your physician far enough in advance of your departure to work out a schedule for any shots you may need—and to allow time to recover from them. Cholera immunization, for example, may make you feel terrible for a few days. Therefore it's a good idea to get it over with early so that you can recuperate before you leave. It is also a good idea to see your dentist and get any necessary work taken care of well ahead of time. A dental emergency overseas can be rather frightening, so it pays to take precautions.

Even better than a visit to your family physician—who may seldom travel and hardly ever sees a rare tropical disease in his or her practice—would be a call or visit to one of the traveler's health clinics that have recently emerged under hospital or medical school auspices in several areas of the United States. These are staffed by medical personnel who are thoroughly knowledgeable about health and sanitary conditions in every part of the world. They can provide pre-trip counseling, immunizations, prescriptions, and post-trip checkups at very reasonable rates. Many of them offer telephone consultation to physicians.

California: Traveler's Clinic, University Medical Center, 225 Dickinson Avenue, San Diego 92110. Telephone (619) 294-5787.

District of Columbia: Traveler's Medical Service of Washington, 2141 K Street, N.W., Washington 20037. Telephone (202) 466-8109.

Florida: Tropical Medicine and Travelers' Clinic, University of Miami Medical School, 1550 NW Tenth Avenue, Miami 33125. Telephone (305) 325-9845.

Louisiana: Travelers Health Clinic, Tulane Medical Center, 1415 Tulane Avenue, New Orleans 70112. Telephone (504) 588-5580.

Massachusetts: Travelers' Clinic, New England Medical Center, 171 Harrison Avenue, Boston 02111. Telephone (617) 956-5811.

New York: The International Health Care Service of The New York Hospital-Cornell Medical Center, 525 East 68 Street, New York 10021. Telephone (212) 472-4284.

Ohio: Travelers Clinic, Division of Geographic Medicine, University Hospitals, Cleveland 44106. Telephone (216) 444-3295.

Pennsylvania: Travelhealth Center, The Medical College of Pennsylvania, 3300 Henry Avenue, Philadelphia 19129. Telephone (215) 842-6465.

Washington: University Hospital Travel and Tropical Medicine Clinic, University of Washington, Seattle 98195. Telephone (206) 543-7191.

Virginia: Travelers Clinic, Division of Geographic Medicine, School of Medicine, Box 485, University of Virginia, Charlottesville 22908. Telephone (804) 924-5241.

## IMMUNIZATIONS

People ask, "What shots are required?" when they should be asking, "What shots do I need besides those that are required?"

If you are going from the United States or Canada to Western Europe or the Caribbean, none are required. There are only two quarantinable diseases for which vaccination certificates are mandatory under the regulations of the World Health Organization: cholera and yellow fever. These certificates consist of entries in the "yellow card"—actually a small booklet that can fit into your passport—attesting to the date and type of vaccination and signed by a supervising physician. (Airlines, travel agents, traveler's health clinics, and U.S. Public Health Service offices distribute them free of charge.) Yellow fever is found in Asia and Africa; cholera in Asia, Africa, the Middle East, and parts of the Pacific. Not every country in those areas is affected, however.

A yellow fever immunization seldom causes any discomfort or side effects and is valid for ten years. It can only be given at an authorized center—a U.S. Public Health Service station or traveler's health clinic—during certain hours of the day because of the fragile nature of the virus. The traveler should be protected against yellow fever in affected countries even if immunization is not required for entry. Cholera shots, on the other hand, cause severe discomfort for several days. Because the shots are only 50 percent effective and last for only six months, the U.S. Public Health Service does not recommend getting them unless they are required for entry into a country. The last case of smallpox anywhere in the world was reported on October 26, 1977. However, in some countries an unvaccinated traveler may encounter an unenlightened health officer at the airport and get jabbed. To forestall this, it is a good idea to get your yellow card stamped "Vaccine not given," or carry a physician's letter stating that you are not to be vaccinated.

Once the World Health Organization requirements are out of the way, most countries are reluctant to admit that they harbor any major diseases. Thus, embassies, consulates, government tourist offices, and airlines are not reliable sources of information about what sort of medical protection you really need. Anyone going to a developing country should have typhoid, gamma globulin, and polio immunization. Polio immunization lasts only five years for the Sabin live virus, three years for the Salk killed virus. In developed countries, you are protected because everyone else is protected, but in other places you are vulnerable. When you go for a polio booster, tell the physician whether your original immunization was Salk or Sabin. If your original shot was Salk or you are over twenty and have never been immunized for polio, you must have a Salk booster or a Salk shot. For the prevention of hepatitis in any place where the water and sanitation are not top quality, gamma globulin and the new hepatitis B vaccine are strongly advised. (Where do you find *top* quality? The United States, Canada, Western Europe, Japan, Australia, New Zealand, Israel, and South Africa.)

Malaria is found in many parts of Africa, Asia, South America, Mexico, and the Caribbean. There is no immunization against the malaria parasite, but you can take precautions to prevent the disease from developing. Starting one week before entering an infected area and continuing for six weeks after leaving it, take chloroquine (available under several trade names), Fansidar, or both in pill form, depending on the type of malaria found in the area. These medications suppress the development of the disease. Your family physician is unlikely to be aware of the various strains of malaria and the medications to which they may be resistant. The U.S. Public Health Service or a traveler's health clinic can advise you or you can consult the excellent World Malaria Risk Chart published by IAMAT. (For more information on IAMAT, see pp. 194–197.)

For an up-to-date report on the latest health conditions and immunization requirements, the World Wide Health Forecast, a service of the International League of Travelers, offers a toll-free hot line with information based on reports from international organizations, including the World Health Organization and the United States State Department. Call (800) 368-3531 between 9:00 A.M. and 6:00 P.M. Eastern Standard Time.

## AIR TRAVEL

To dry out or not to dry out—that's an important question for wheelchair travelers because lavatory facilities on airplanes are cramped (and getting smaller as the planes get bigger) and difficult to get to. Patty Hughes says, "I don't drink a thing for twelve hours before an airplane trip." Carr Massi says, "We don't go the the bathroom." Margery McMullin, director of the New York Easter Seal Home Service found that among a group of handicapped teenagers she escorted to Japan, "the girls could dry themselves out, but the boys couldn't."

What is the medical opinion? "Don't do it," says Dr. Maynard I. Shapiro of Chicago's Jackson Park Hospital. "The humidity in an airplane is less than five percent and your body requires moisture to counter ozone irritation." It's best to drink small quantities of water, soft drinks, and fruit juices constantly throughout a plane trip, exactly the same thing that the airline crew does. You can cut down the bathroom visits by avoiding tea and alcohol, both of which act as diuretics.

## FOOD ON THE PLANE

You don't have to eat it just because it is set in front of you. Don't eat more than you would at home and don't eat something you're not accustomed to—you can experiment with new dishes when you arrive at your destination. On the plane it it wise to keep your stomach soothed and not overly full. Many people find that cheese and orange juice (not necessarily together!) can be upsetting; so if you have a queasy stomach, it is best to avoid them. Grapefruit and tomato juice are usually available for breakfast.

## EXERCISE ON THE PLANE

This can be your best defense against many of the symptoms that are usually attributed to "jet lag." Dr. Ludwig G. Lederer, medical director of American Airlines for seventeen years, is a firm believer in the value of doing isometrics while in flight. So is Juergen Palm, head of the German Sports Federation, who devised a series of in-flight exercises for Lufthansa German Airlines. They are described in a free booklet called *Fitness in the Chair*, which you can get by sending a self-addressed long envelope (no stamp necessary) to Dept. UX12, Lufthansa German Airlines, 1640 Hempstead Turnpike, East Meadow, New York 11554. SAS also offers a free flyer called *Exercise in the Chair*, which illustrates eight exercises devised by the company's medical adviser, Folke Mossfeldt. Write for it to SAS, Box EX, 138-02 Queens Boulevard, Jamaica, New York 11435.

The idea of doing exercises while airborne started with the American astronauts when it was discovered in the space program how important it was to maintain good muscle tone and cardiovascular fitness on prolonged flights. Even when not heading for the moon, body functions slow down significantly on long flights. The heartbeat rate drops, reducing the supply of oxygen to the blood. The joints stiffen and muscles lose their tone. As a result, the passenger feels exhausted just at the moment he has to pull himself together for disembarking and encountering a strange place. Doing isometric exercises—which merely means tightening and relaxing various muscles of the body without actually moving—helps maintain muscle tone and circulation. Dr. Lederer, who is an authority on aerospace medicine, comments that the exercises often prescribed for people confined to wheelchairs are excellent for combating travel fatigue.

## FOOD AND WATER ABROAD

I once heard a Boston lady warn her daughter, who was about to leave for a trip to Texas, "Now, dear, remember not to drink the water or eat any raw fruits or vegetables." She apparently hadn't heard that the Lone Star State had joined the Union and her concern was misplaced, but in a general way she did have the right idea.

Certainly, in most major cities there is no problem. Travelers are more often felled with stomach upsets by the strangeness of food and water, by overexhaustion, and by nervous tension than by contamination. On a tour of seven West African countries, for example, only two out of thirty-four people became ill—one when she lost her purse, the other when her luggage went astray. Both recovered as soon as their possessions were found.

There are some places where you need to take precautions. Mexico is probably the prime example, as well as some parts of Asia, Africa, and South America. In these places, not only do you not drink tap water, you don't even brush your teeth with it. Use only bottled water, preferably carbonated, and be sure you get a sealed bottle. Don't use ice in your drinks. You might like to cultivate a taste for beer, which is always safe; sweet soft drinks are a perfect culture for bacteria that may be present in a not-too-sanitary bottling plant. Don't eat salads and only eat fruit that you peel yourself. Avoid milk, dairy products and mayonnaise. It is safe, however, to assume that hot food and beverages made with boiled water are all right.

## THE TOURIST'S SCOURGE

Having taken all possible precautions, you may nevertheless come down with *turista*, "Montezuma's Revenge," "The Green Death," or whatever you want to call it—that awful combination of diarrhea, cramps, chills, and fever that strikes like lightning. (And it sometimes strikes in unexpected places.) As with seasickness, the worst of it is that it doesn't kill you, you just suffer. What to do? The best and most convenient remedy is Lomotil in tablet form. It is a prescription drug, so be sure to mention it to your doctor before you leave home. The tablets are tiny and even one can be remarkably effective, though it's usually necessary to take several to stop all the symptoms. Kaopectate and Pargel, which are liquids, are also good, but a nuisance to carry when traveling. Pepto-Bismol is equally effective and available in tablet form.

Even when the symptoms are gone, you will feel weak because of dehydration. Your body needs to replace vital fluids and electrolytes, but just drinking water will not do the trick. The Federal Centers for Disease Control provide a simple recipe for getting your body back in sync after a bout of tourist's diarrhea. Here it is.

> Take two glasses. In one glass put eight ounces of orange juice, half a teaspoon of honey, corn syrup or sugar and a pinch of table salt. In the second glass put eight ounces of carbonated or boiled water and a quarter teaspoon of baking soda. Drink alternately from each glass. Supplement these liquids with carbonated beverages, boiled water or hot tea. Avoid solid foods and milk until you have fully recovered. If you are diabetic or on a salt-restricted diet, ask your doctor if it would be all right to use this formula. If not, your physician may be able to suggest substitute ingredients that would have the same effect.

An improvement over this simple home remedy is a product called "Dialyte." It's a formulation of oral rehydration salts, which, dissolved in water (boiled, of course!), replaces the body's lost liquid and minerals. Not for sale, Dialyte is available at no charge to members of IAMAT (pp. 194–197).

## KIDNEY DISEASE

There are more than forty thousand people in the world who have received kidney transplants and many thousands more on dialysis who spend several hours a day several days a week hooked up to machines that cleanse their blood so they can live. Before the advent of these techniques, none of them would have survived. But there is more to life than survival. Kidney patients are beginning to realize—as other disabled people have for some time—that it may be possible to live almost normally within the constraints of a handicapping condition.

Kidney patients can now travel, with their physician's approval, to other cities and countries and maintain their dialysis routine at hospitals and renal centers that are willing to make arrangements for transient patients. In all the centers ample prior application is necessary. A physician's summary and recommendations for treatment are required, as well as the recent result of the Australia Antigen test. If travel plans are canceled, it is important to notify the host unit because regular patients may have modified their routines in order to help transients that were expected and a "no show," besides being rude, would disrupt scheduling and personnel assignments.

The National Association of Patients on Hemodialysis and Transplantation (NAPHT) publishes a Guide to International Dialysis in its quarterly journal, indicating, among other information, the type of dialysis offered at each center. Write NAPHT, 150 Nassau Street, New York, New York 10038. Telephone (212) 619-2727.

## RESPIRATORY AILMENTS

Anyone with a respiratory problem should ask his or her physician about the advisability of flying. The extremely low humidity in an airplane may cause discomfort. Altitude should not be a problem, since all commercial planes are certified to 7,500 feet—that is, even though you may be 30,000 feet in the air, the pressure inside the plane is the same as it would be 7,500 feet above the ground. Regulations affecting oxygen-powered respirators are discussed in chapter 1, Air Travel. Some people use corset-type respirators that operate on dry-cell batteries, which are permissible on an aircraft. A respirator with a compressor that plugs into house current is fine within the United States, where 110- to 120-volt current is almost universal, but the traveler must be able to do without the respirator for the length of his intended airplane trip plus a couple of hours' leeway in case of delay in takeoff or landing. Anyone who wants to take such a respirator and compressor to foreign countries, however, needs a brief course on the subject of electricity.

Let's start with an object lesson. Pearl R, who uses a thirty-pound respirator with a compressor, refused to stay behind when her husband went to Kenya to lead a photo safari. He knew something about electricity and told her that most foreign current operates on 220 volts. So she went to the local hardware store and bought a cute litte three-ounce converter that brings 220 volts down to 110-120 volts, plus a package of plugs and adapters that would fit various types of wall outlets found overseas. The appliance—in this case, the respirator—plugs into the converter, which can be plugged into a wall outlet in some countries or has the appropriate adapter plug snapped onto it for use in other countries.

Pearl used her apparatus for the first time in London's Heathrow Airport, where it overheated, sparked, and sputtered but didn't give up. She next plugged it in at the Inter-Continental Hotel in Nairobi, where the adapter blew a fuse and the voltage converter ceased functioning entirely. A friend loaned her a heavy-duty transformer that she had brought along for her hair dryer. It was actually underrated for the respirator, but it held up for the rest of the trip and Pearl got home safe and happy.

What went wrong? Those three-ounce converters are fine for heating appliances without motors, such as irons, hair curlers and stylers, and coffee-cup heaters. But any appliance with a motor—and that includes hair dryers and electric shavers—requires a heavy-duty converter, sometimes called a transformer. The converter wattage should always equal that of the appliance. Since Pearl's respirator was rated at 3.5

amps, and wattage is determined by multiplying amps times volts, its output was 420 watts. Therefore, what she needed was a 500-watt, heavy-duty converter. (If a converter of the exact size isn't available, always use the next larger, never smaller.)

No one should take chances with a life-or-death piece of equipment like a respirator. Heavy-duty converters are manufactured by Todd Systems, Inc., 50 Ash Street, Yonkers, New York 10701 (telephone [914] 963-3400).

For small appliances without motors, the Franzus Company (352 Park Avenue South, New York, New York 10010) sells converters and adapters as well as dual-voltage (110/ 220 v) travel care products. There is some helpful advice in the company's free booklet, *Foreign Electricity Is No Dark Secret.* Parks Products, 3511 Cahuenga, Hollywood, California 90068, also supplies converters, transformers, and adapter plugs for small appliances.

## MEDICAL SERVICES ORGANIZATIONS
## TO HELP THE TRAVELER

**Air Medic,** 12517 Chandler Boulevard, North Hollywood, California 91607; toll-free telephone: (800) 423-2667; in California: (213) 985-2020. Air Medic is a private company that supplies medical services to air travelers. It has three hundred planes all over the United States under contract to provide air ambulance service with adequate facilities—important to know about since there are no government regulations covering air ambulances, and as a result, any plane can be so termed even though it may not carry a doctor, nurse, or medical equipment. In addition, Air Medic can arrange for nurses, inhalation therapists and physicians. It can also make transportation arrangements and coordinate an entire trip. If a passenger becomes ill on a plane, Air Medic can put his or her own doctor or one of its panel of aerospace physicians on aeronautical radio from any place in the country to a plane anywhere over the United States and some other parts of the world. This is one of the companies that can supply oxygen packed to FAA specifications for use in flight or as cargo. Air Medic works only for individuals, not the airlines, and is frequently used by travel agents.

**Intermedic, Inc.,** 777 Third Avenue, New York, New York 10017; telephone (212) 486-8900. Intermedic is an international network of English-speaking physicians who are pledged to respond to emergency calls from members and to abide by the following schedule of rates for initial visits:

| | |
|---|---|
| Office visit | US$30–$40 |
| House or hotel visit | |
| Day (7:00 A.M.–7:00 P.M.) | US$40–$50 |
| Night (7:00 P.M.–7:00 A.M.) | US$50–$60 |

Members receive the *Intermedic Directory*, which lists participating physicians in over two hundred cities and ninety countries. Home as well as office telephone numbers are included. The directory contains a personal medical data section for listing pertinent information that would help a doctor treating the patient overseas. Member physicians will recommend suitable physicians in nearby communities for which no listings are given. Members may also make use of Intermedic's overseas health information service, which answers questions about immunizations and medication. Cost of membership is $6 a year for a personal membership and $10 for a family membership.

**International Association for Medical Assistance to Travelers (IAMAT),** 736 Center Street, Lewiston, New York

14092. Telephone (716) 754-4883. In Canada, 1287 St. Clair Avenue West, Toronto, Ont. M6E 1B8. IAMAT is a nonprofit foundation created to provide medical assistance to travelers in distress and to coordinate medical procedures all over the world. Membership is free. The organization is financed by donations that are tax-deductible in both the United States and Canada.

Members receive a sixty-four-page directory listing IAMAT centers in 450 cities in 120 countries and the names and addresses of individual English-speaking physicians associated with IAMAT. Any such center will furnish the names of approved English-speaking doctors from a panel that is on duty twenty-four hours a day. The doctors have agreed to abide by the following schedule of rates (unless otherwise noted in the directory):

| | |
|---|---|
| Office | US$20 |
| House call (hotels etc.) | US$30 |
| Night call (10:00 P.M. to 7:00 A.M.) and Sundays and local holidays | US$35 |

A membership card is issued for identification. Members receive a world immunization and malaria risk chart that answers every question a traveler might have about these subjects. They also get a handy personal clinical record form on which they or their physicians can note emergency medical data; eyeglass prescriptions; immunization records, diabetes, cardiovascular and allergy information; and the physician's diagnostic summary. Members also receive a free packet of Dialyte oral rehydration salts (see "The Tourist's Scourge," pp. 189–190) and can request additional packets at no charge. It is well worth making a donation to IAMAT in order to receive a special bonus available only to contributors: a set of twenty-four climate charts covering the entire world except for Antarctica. They contain details on specific climatic conditions throughout the year, advice on clothing, and information on the sanitary condition of water, food, and milk in 1,440 cities around the world. IAMAT is thoughtful enough to use both U.S. and metric measures as well as Fahrenheit and Celsius temperatures. All the information is coded so that it fits into a very small space. The following is a sample, decoded:

> Palermo, Sicily, Italy, 31 meters/102 feet above sea level. The water is chlorinated and has no ill effect on local people. However, some strains of *E. coli*, a main component of the bacterial population of the bowel, are at times present in very small concentrations in all potable water. Some local strains are different than those that we are accustomed to and may cause diarrhea in those people who, like visitors, could not develop immunity because of short exposure. A safe course for the first few weeks is to drink bottled water. The milk is pasteurized and safe to drink. Butter, cheese and ice cream are safe. Local meat, poultry, sea food, vegetables and fruits are safe to eat. In January the highest average temperature is 16 Celsius/61 Fahrenheit, the lowest average is 8 Celsius/46 Fahrenheit. The mean relative humidity is 72 percent and the average number of days with precipitation is 12. Light wool suits or dresses, sweaters, with lightweight topcoat for evenings. Rainwear advisable.

What more could anyone want to know?

IAMAT also publishes *How to Adapt to Altitude, How to Avoid Traveler's Diarrhea, Personal Health in Warm Coun-*

*tries, How to Protect Yourself Against Malaria,* and *World Malaria Risk Chart.*

There's an interesting sidelight about the origin of IAMAT. It was founded by an Italian cardiologist, Dr. Vincenzo Marcolongo (now its president), after he had been involved in treating a young tourist from the United States who fell gravely ill after taking aminopyrine as a pain-relieving agent following a tooth extraction. The dentist who had prescribed the drug didn't know that aminopyrine, which is a popular aspirin substitute in parts of Europe, can be dangerous and even fatal to people of Anglo-Saxon or Scandinavian descent. That's how Dr. Marcolongo became interested in medical problems related to international travel.

**Medic Alert Foundation International,** P.O. Box 1009, Turlock, California 95381. Telephone (800) 344-3226; in California (800) 468-1020. Medic Alert is a nonprofit organization that provides an emergency medical identification system for treatment of health conditions which may not easily be seen or recognized. In return for a fee of $20, members receive a lifetime membership in the foundation and three potentially life-saving benefits.

The first of these is a metal disk attached to a necklace or bracelet that bears the insignia of the medical profession and the words "Medic Alert" in red. On the other side are engraved the wearer's chief medical problem, his membership number and the telephone number of Medic Alert's emergency answering service. This disk is meant to be worn whenever the member is away from home in order to alert emergency personnel to the fact that he has a health problem they should know about.

The member also receives a wallet card containing personal and medical information in addition to that on the emblem. The card is reissued and updated with current information every year, or at any time the member desires. Every year he receives a computer printout of all such information so that he can be sure it is accurate.

The emergency answering service is the third part of the system. That phone number, engraved on the member's disk, can be called collect from anyplace in the world. Within seconds of receiving a call, emergency operators can relay information from the member's data file that might save his life. Spanish and French interpreters are always available.

What medical problems are not obvious? Here are the most common ones, in order of prevalence:

1. allergic to penicillin
2. diabetes/insulin dependent
3. diabetes/diet controlled
4. taking anticoagulants
5. heart condition
6. wearing contact lenses
7. allergic to sulfa
8. epilepsy
9. allergic to insect stings
10. allergic to bee stings
11. asthma
12. allergic to codeine
13. glaucoma
14. allergic to tetanus toxoid
15. allergic to aspirin
16. taking cortisone
17. hypoglycemia
18. organ donor
19. neck breather (laryngectomy)
20. implanted pacemaker
21. allergic to morphine
22. allergic to Demerol
23. allergic to novocaine
24. emphysema
25. multidrug allergies
26. hemophilia
27. allergic to tetracyclines
28. allergic to antibiotics
29. hypertension
30. multiple sclerosis
31. Addison's disease
32. myasthenia gravis
33. allergic to Terramycin
34. allergic to barbiturates
35. allergic to I.V.P. dyes

36. allergic to cortisone
37. allergic to phenobarbital
38. takes steroids
39. adrenal insufficiency
40. kidney transplant
41. allergic to sulfonamides

42. allergic to salicylates
43. takes B-blocker
44. Alzheimer's disease
45. coronary artery bypass graft (CABG)
46. malignant hyperthermia

And there are 153 other not uncommon conditions that have prompted people to join Medic Alert!

In any part of the world, the identification disk is easily noticed when an unconscious person or one unable to communicate in the local language is being examined for injury. New York City police look for a Medic Alert disk even before they search a wallet for identification.

# 8

# TRAVEL TIPS

There is a right way and a wrong way to do everything. In travel, the right way is whatever works for you—your needs, your tastes, your own particular idiosyncrasies. But there are many things that professional travelers have learned, often through bitter experience, which can ease the way for others and simplify what might appear to be complicated problems.

## LUGGAGE AND PACKING

Not for nothing are airport baggage handlers more commonly known as "baggage smashers." Keep that in mind when shopping for luggage. Whatever you get should be sturdy, well constructed, and not very expensive. If you fall in love with a fragile, high-fashion suitcase, you will have your heart broken when you see what it looks like emerging from the baggage chute. It doesn't pay to get emotionally involved with luggage. Nor is it much of an economy to borrow it— the lender may be unexpectedly miffed at the dents, scuffs, and stains that inevitably accumulate on even the shortest trip. It is wisest to buy your own luggage in the medium-price range, where you get durability without faddishness.

Soft-sided or hard-sided? This may be as much a matter of personality as of practicality. Soft luggage is probably more popular because it is very lightweight and you can stuff it and stuff it—until it's very heavy. The nice thing about soft luggage is that there is always room for purchases acquired on a trip as well as for homeward-bound dirty laundry, which—according to some remarkable law of physics—always takes up more space than the same items did when they were clean. The drawback to soft luggage is that your clothes will get wrinkled—unless you happen to be adept at the army method of packing a B-4 bag by *rolling* the clothes instead of folding them.

Clothes that are neatly packed with plenty of tissue paper come out of hard-sided luggage almost wrinkle-free. Since you can't do any stuffing, there is no temptation to pack unnecessary items just because "there's a little more room." Hard sides also provide protection against water damage, in case, as sometimes happens, luggage is left standing on a rainy airfield during loading or unloading. My personal preference is for Halliburton aluminum cases, which are lightweight, indestructible, as utilitarian-looking as a Jeep, and cost the earth. Less expensive, but solid and quite attractive is the molded luggage made by such companies as American Tourister and Samsonite.

Whatever type of luggage you choose, be sure to put some identification *inside* the bag. Airlines supply labels that will stick to the lining; you can also drop in a business card or a piece of your own printed stationery. The reason is that outside baggage tags can be lost. If this happens, the bag will be opened in hope of finding the owner's identity. Be sure to include your home address and your destination address on inside and outside tags. *Remove old baggage tags.* It isn't sophisticated to leave them on, just confusing.

At least 90 percent of all luggage falls into a few standard sizes and styles. To make yours easier to identify in terminals and hotel lobbies, stick a strip of masking tape in a sharply contrasting color diagonally from top to bottom corners on *both sides* of your suitcase. Keep one key to it in your pocket or purse, another in your small overnight bag as a backup.

One suitcase to be checked as baggage plus a flight bag or something similar for immediate needs is enough luggage for anybody going anywhere. The flight bag should contain overnight requisites, medication, and anything you might need on the plane. Joni Eareckson says, "I take on board one travel case which is filled with all the essentials I might need in an emergency—catheters and things like that. The plane might be delayed, so if anything happens I'll have all my things handy."

When deciding what to take, first write down everything you think you will need, keeping in mind the weather and program in store for you. Then revise the list, eliminating duplications (you do not need two evening purses or two tweed jackets) and making sure that everything goes together in one basic color scheme. Lay it all out on the bed; take a long, hard look, then put half the stuff back in the closet.

Everything you take should have a specific function—for warmth, for coolness, for dress-up, etc.—but look askance at anything that is "just for a change." And don't buy new clothes for a trip unless there is something you really need. You will be meeting new people all the time who won't know that you're wearing your old clothes. Besides, you should be familiar with the characteristics and quirks of everything you take along. A foreign country is no place to discover that a zipper doesn't work properly or that a drip-dry shirt isn't color-fast.

Put all liquids, whether cosmetics or medication, into plastic containers and seal the caps with tape. Keep some extra tape with you for the return trip. Fill containers no more than halfway to allow for expansion in the air. For the same reason, never pack a full aerosol can. Do not put lighter fluid, matches, or anything flammable into checked luggage.

NEVER PACK YOUR PASSPORT IN A SUITCASE. That might seem childishly obvious, but it wasn't long ago that a prominent travel agent caused an international incident by doing that very thing as she tried to cross a border while her passport lay in a suitcase five hundred miles away. Keep your passport in your pocketbook or inside coat pocket at all times. Don't check it in a hotel safe because you will need it to cash traveler's checks. In some countries you may have to leave your passport at the hotel desk for a few hours or overnight. This is a police regulation. Be sure to ask for it if it isn't returned to you promptly.

Put two or three wire hangers into the bottom of your suitcase. European hotels never give you enough hangers and in the newer places the hangers don't have hooks, so you can't hang them over the shower rod for drip-drying. Inexpensive foam rubber covers, available in five-and-tens, fit over wire hangers to keep rust stains off wet clothes. European skirt hangers only work with skirts that have sewn-in loops, but some large safety pins will convert the wire hangers into skirt hangers.

Pack suits, coats, dresses, skirts, and blouses in the plastic garment bags that dry cleaners use. The air trapped inside the bag acts as a cushion and helps to prevent wrinkles. Pack shoes in old stretch socks, not in plastic, which seals in moisture and could damage them. Men's shirts should have the laundry cardboard removed and a couple of socks tucked around the collars to keep them from getting crushed.

A useful trick for men is to roll up a package of underwear, socks, and handkerchiefs for every day of the trip. Put these rolls into plastic bags and use them as padding around other clothing. Getting dressed is simplified when you just pull one of the packages out of your suitcase or bureau drawer, without having to noodle around for a handkerchief or the other brown sock. A couple of additional plastic bags are handy for wet bathing suits or laundry that didn't quite dry in time for an early-morning departure.

Neckties can be rolled or wrapped around shirt cardboards and secured with rubber bands. Knitted neckties and ready-made bow ties are excellent for travel. Shirts with French cuffs should be left at home—it is too easy to lose or mislay the cuff links.

Women need only two pocketbooks—one for travel and day use, one for evening that folds flat in a suitcase. The evening bag should be large enough for passport, wallet, traveler's checks, and eyeglasses. If you can get along with only one pocketbook, so much the better.

As you pack your suitcase, write down everything that goes in. Leave one copy at home, take another one with you. This list serves two important functions. First, you can refer to it when you are checking out of hotels to be sure that everything has been packed. (Be sure to add to the list any purchases you make abroad.) Second, on the rare chance that your suitcase should be lost in transit, this list provides proof of the value of your loss to the airline or insurance company. It is almost impossible to reconstruct from memory the contents of a lost suitcase and it will be to your detriment if you cannot provide an accurate accounting.

## COMFORT IN THE AIR

Wear loose, comfortable clothing. If it is going to be a long trip, remove belt, necktie, jewelry, and hairpins and put them where you can reach them easily for disembarkation. Take off your shoes and put on soft slippers or airline-type socks (you can buy them for less than a dollar in variety stores). Remember to have a shoehorn with you for putting your shoes back on. *Everybody* swells up on airplanes in one place or another, usually in the feet or ankles.

It can get very chilly in the cabin and a sweater is useful because it is not constricting. An all-wool sweater is best because it gives you the most warmth with the least weight. A cashmere cardigan is ideal, so if anyone wants to give you a handsome—and expensive—going-away present, you know what to ask for.

Experienced travelers keep their seat belts loosely fastened all the time. You will be warned of any impending turbulence, of course, but sometimes there are little bumps and lurches that make it reassuring to be strapped in.

Enjoy yourself but watch the food and drink. A cocktail or a glass of wine is a festive, relaxing way to start a trip, but one is enough. Alcohol is a diuretic and there is no reason to be confronted with the bathroom problem more than necessary. It also dries up the throat membranes—the last thing anyone needs in the bone-dry atmosphere of an airplane cabin. Eat moderately—remember that you are expending hardly any energy for several hours.

Whether to take any medication for motion sickness is something to be discussed with your physician. Most such preparations cause drowsiness. You might be interested to know that many people who feel uncomfortable during take-offs, landings, or turbulence find that antacid tablets such as

Gelusil, Camalox, Mylanta, and others, are very effective. Since all of these contain ingredients that are not permitted on some diets, ask your doctor if it is all right to use them.

## JET LAG

This is the discrepancy between the time on local clocks and the time your body says it is back home. It may be 8:00 A.M. in London and time to get up for breakfast, but your body *knows* that it is really only 3:00 A.M. and you need to finish your night's sleep. Aerospace scientists have figured that it takes one whole day to adjust to each time zone a traveler crosses—that is, every time you have to move your watch an hour, you are going to need twenty-four hours to adjust your internal clock. It isn't as bad as it may sound. What happens is that you may be a little foggy for a few days and tend to be sleepy or wide awake at odd hours.

Avoidance of overeating and overdrinking will help, as well as taking naps whenever it is convenient. Taking some aspirin or aspirin substitute may make you feel more comfortable, but the most important thing is simply to relax and let your body adjust at its own rate. The one thing that makes jet lag much easier to take is flying during the day so that you arrive at the right time to go to bed, get a good night's sleep and get up at about the same time as everyone else. There are very few flights to Europe during the day and tours never seem to use them, but for an independent traveler they offer a little extra comfort at no additional cost.

## CLOTHING

People probably worry more about what to wear than any other single aspect of a trip, men just as much as women. This isn't frivolous. Besides practical considerations of keeping warm, cool, or dry, there is the very human desire to do the right thing, to fit in with the surrounding culture, and to present one's best and most attractive self to the world.

Handicapped people are no different from anyone else in this regard. Joni Eareckson comments, "Just because I'm handicapped I don't have to look like it. I have to keep healthy, exercise my arms, keep my weight at a good level, and care about my appearance." And Joni has succeeded, because she is lovely to look at.

Men always seem to look fine. Since their clothes consist of pants, shirt, and jacket or sweater, the only variations possible are in color and fabric, according to personal taste. For traveling, they need only to select whatever is suitable for the climate they are going to and make sure they have one conservative outfit for evening wear. Teenagers, even though they are handicapped, are just as uniform—they wear exactly what their able-bodied contemporaries wear and that is as it should be.

But women have so many options open to them in clothing and so many choices to make that it is no wonder they sometimes err in the direction of choosing what their friends are wearing rather than what is best for them.

In a wide-angle photograph of 109 members of a tour at Honolulu airport, one fashion note is striking. Women in wheelchairs look more attractive in long skirts or pants than they do in short skirts. When you think about it, *most* women sitting down look better in long skirts or pants. Short skirts ride up, wrinkle, stretch across the thighs, and generally have an unkempt appearance. Pants have many advantages, especially for people who are sensitive to cold, but they should be cut generously to avoid wrinkles.

For evening, any woman in a wheelchair should seize the opportunity to wear long skirts. With skirts and blouses in various fabrics, this kind of outfit can be casual, formal, or anything in between. A wonderful wrap for day or evening is the newly popular shawl, much more graceful and easy to handle than a jacket. Interesting shawls are fun to shop for abroad. Long wool skirts with matching shawls are high fashion and perfect for a woman confined to a wheelchair. A home sewer can make an outfit like this very easily. Black ballet slippers (the professional dancer's kind) are soft, comfortable, and attractive—as well as inexpensive—but are not suitable for a person who does any walking at all.

For cold weather, a heavy poncho is more comfortable and better-looking than a coat or even a short jacket. (Men can wear these, too.) Short capes are practical wraps that can be run off at home or by a dressmaker if they are not available in stores. One of the best ways to stay warm in a cold climate without filling up luggage with heavy clothing is to get underwear made of sheer wool or polypropylene, a synthetic yarn that draws moisture away from the skin. It takes up not much more room in a suitcase than a couple of handkerchiefs, and under a shirt or blouse will keep you as warm as a heavy sweater would.

In hot climates try to wear all-natural fiber fabrics rather than synthetics. Natural fibers let your skin breathe and keep you much cooler. In *really* hot climates, wear only cotton underwear. It is hard to find nowadays, but worth searching for if you are going to a place that is hot and humid.

Special clothing for people who are confined to wheelchairs or who have trouble getting into ordinary garments

can be ordered by mail from Vocational Guidance and Rehabilitation Services, 2239 East 55th Street, Cleveland, Ohio
44103; telephone (216) 431-7800. They make clothing and
underwear for men and women. The selection available for
women starts with a basic back-wrapped dress for $25. For
a catalogue, send $1 to the Sewing Department at the afore-
mentioned address.

Farther afield, in Japan a store called Tahira Shokai caters
to many needs of the handicapped and sells everything from
underwear, pajamas, and other clothing to bathtubs and
wheelchairs. The address is 2-31 Takamatsu, Toshima-ku,
Tokyo. A branch store is located at 2-1-2 Miyahara, Yodo-
gawa-ku, Osaka. Also in Osaka is a boutique called Helpers
in the basement of the Hanshin Hotel. It features women's
clothing designed by Namiko Mori, a prominent Japanese
fashion designer. Mannequins in wheelchairs display her styles
for the handicapped.


## MONEY


When going abroad, take almost all your money in traveler's
checks. You can get them free at Barclays Bank; there is a
1 percent charge at most other banks. Get them in $10 and
$20 denominations. Make a note of the check numbers and
keep it in a different place from where you keep the checks.
Leave a copy of the list of check numbers at home.

You get a better rate of exchange if you convert your
money at your destination rather than at home, but it is a
good idea to get about $10 in foreign currency, which you
are going to need on arrival for things like tips and taxis. Many
banks offer prepacks of foreign currency in small amounts
and denominations. Study the currency on the plane going

over and learn to identify the coins and bills. If you buy a drink on the plane, ask for your change in the currency of the country you are going to.

Always change money at a bank or exchange office (*cambio* and *wechsel* are the words to look for) for the best rate. Hotels, restaurants, and stores may change it for you as a courtesy, but they take a whopping fee for doing so. Try to figure out how much money you will need for a few days at a time and change just that much. Avoid having to change much foreign currency back into dollars because you always lose on the deal. Keep some American money and small change in a separate purse to use for taxis and telephone calls on your return home. Remember that *coins* cannot be exchanged anywhere, so don't get stuck with too many foreign ones at the end of a trip, unless you want them for souvenirs or expect to go back to that country. On the other hand, keep enough coins for tips when you leave a country because the porter can't exchange coins either and a few quarters won't do him any good.

# AFTERWORD

It was in Hong Kong a few years ago that the first edition of *Access to the World* had its genesis. While waiting in the crowded, noisy Star Ferry Terminal to board one of the toylike ferryboats that constantly ply the harbor between Hong Kong and Kowloon on the China mainland, I saw an attractive, well-dressed woman pushing a very pretty younger woman, about twenty years old, in a wheelchair. They were obviously mother and daughter and, just as obviously, Americans.

They waited while some porters opened the turnstiles leading to the gangplank so that the wheelchair could go through. Then they went up the gangplank to the deck and positioned themselves near the rail where they could get the best view of the bustling harbor.

Just like any other tourists, I thought. And then I realized that, of course, they were like any other tourists. They had flown a long distance or, perhaps, taken a cruise ship. They were staying in a hotel, eating in restaurants, shopping, sightseeing. Certainly, they were able to afford an expensive vacation. But what was more important was the fact that they were doing exactly what they would have been doing had the daughter not been disabled. And that started me thinking about how many more people like them there must be.

Later, I learned about the handicapped people who travel on business. I met a young woman who had hitchhiked around Australia in a wheelchair. I heard about a couple, both paraplegics, who were sailing a boat around the world by themselves. Example followed example of courageous, determined people who treated their handicaps the way a golfer treats his handicap—he may have to overcome a few strokes but he's in the game to win.

Not everyone is an adventurer or a daredevil. But there are many, many handicapped people who face small adventures every day of their lives as they carry on the normal affairs of work and play that the able-bodied world takes for granted. It is for these people that *Access to the World* was originally written and, thanks to the welcome response it received, that this third edition has been published. I am encouraged to believe that more people need it now not only because more handicapped individuals are traveling but also because the travel industry has recognized this fact and is trying to become more sensitive to their needs and to serve them in practical ways. Armed with information and determination, a new segment of the traveling public is on the move.

# INDEX

Titles of all publications appear in *italic* type.